THE LEEN VALLEY AT WORK

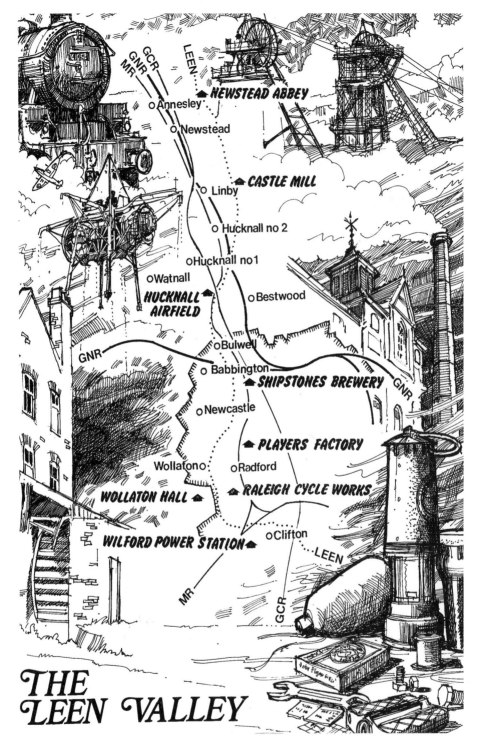

THE LEEN VALLEY

Illustration courtesy of John Michael Webster, the Chatterley Gallery, Eastwood, Notts.

THE LEEN VALLEY
AT WORK
1785-1985

by

Martin R. Weiss

Wharncliffe Publishing Limited

First published in 1996 by
Wharncliffe Publishing Limited

Copyright © Martin R. Weiss

For up-to-date information on other titles produced
under the Wharncliffe imprint, please telephone or
write to:

Wharncliffe Publishing Limited
FREEPOST
47 Church Street
Barnsley
South Yorkshire S70 2BR
Telephone: (24 hours) 01226 734555

ISBN: 871647 34 7

A CIP catalogue record of this book is available from the British
Library.

Printed in Great Britain by
Redwood Books Limited, Trowbridge, Wiltshire

CONTENTS

DEDICATION

In the summer of 1953 my mother hoisted me onto the 'dickey' seat of her Elswick Hopper bicycle and pedalled off with her four-year-old passenger into the midst of the Leen Valley with its meadows, mills, pits and railways. I was fascinated by it all though I never dreamed I would one day write a book about the district. But here it is and it is entirely appropriate that I should dedicate it to Joan Edith Weiss (neé Bell) for giving me my first chance to see the Leen Valley at work.

Rolls Royce Limited, Hucknall. August 28, 1945.
Development Section fitters.

Back Row (left to right) Ron Pressley, Maurice Levers, Henry Green, Arthur Herberts,
Jack Greensmith (Chargehand), Jonnie Cooper (Asst. Chargehand), Ted Brook,
Roy Jefferies, Ken Bostock, Bernard Shaw, Fred Oliver, Harry Patterson (Inspector).

Middle row (left to right) Eddie Beresford, Jack Farnsworth, Frank Wright,
Charles Clements, Chris Garratt, Harry Chapman, V. Read.

Front row (left to right) Peter Moss, Roy Greenhalgh, Walter Owen (Labourer),
Harry Shaw, George Anderson, Herbert Brown, Derek Yapp.

Photo: Stan Grainger/Rolls Royce Heritage

ACKNOWLEDGEMENTS

To the many who helped – in however small a way – during the preparation of this book: Thank You. In particular my special thanks to the following for their ongoing encouragement: Roger & Chris Knowles who first suggested the idea, Ray Mills, Geoff Clarke, Colin Gibson, Stan Grainger, Peter Binns, Eric Horriben, Julie Beer, Malcolm Castledine, David Swale, Tony Hill and John Archer. Also special thanks to Joan Bray, and her staff, at the local studies library, Angel Row, Nottingham and to Eleanor Lingwood at Hucknall local studies library for their valuable help sourcing many of the photographs reproduced here. Finally I would like to acknowledge the work of earlier writers whose efforts helped to enhance my own text.

Martin R. Weiss,
November, 1996.

Introduction

DURING the mid-nineteenth century the small Nottinghamshire towns and villages strung out along the banks of the River Leen between Newstead in the north down to Lenton near the River Trent underwent a transformation. Communities which had for centuries relied upon farming, forestry and milling for a livelihood suddenly found themselves thrust into the industrial revolution which had already swept into many other parts of the British Isles.

It meant that places like Annesley, Newstead, Hucknall, Bulwell, Basford and Lenton were quickly to move out of their medieval time warp and say goodbye to their rural routines. Coal mining, already an established industry at nearby Wollaton since the seventeenth century, was poised by the mid-nineteenth to transform the landscape and social infrastructure of the Leen Valley.

Hucknall, for example, which for centuries had aspired to nothing greater than small village status suddenly developed into an expanding town as new families arrived in the area to settle close to the pits where plenty of jobs were attracting men from miles away ... some, it is said, from as far away as the south of England.

As the Leen Valley coalfield map was established so too was a new way of life that would envelop the district for a century or more. Pits were sunk, chimney stacks sprouted and railway lines spread about the district in a tangle as the old private companies laid down routes to tap the new coal-carrying business.

Nor was it just big business ventures likes mines and railways that got in on this new act. Towns swelling with newcomers meant plenty of opportunities for small-time entrepreneurs too. Britain has always been called a nation of shopkeepers and the Leen Valley provided plenty of scope for the small trader.

The knock-on effect of all this development was dramatic. From Annesley at the very head of the valley with its rows of Welsh-style miners' cottages and Newstead Colliery village with its stark red-brick terraces down through Hucknall and Bulwell with their late Victorian/early Edwardian pocket-size villas the historical records suggest housing developers enjoyed a boom that would make today's builders green with envy. It is no exaggeration to say that the modern appearance of the Leen Valley towns was formed in the period 1860-1913 ... years when building of all types went on unabated. Bricklayers swarmed into the district along with the newly recruited miners. Up went buildings with such diverse uses as waterworks, railway stations, schools, pubs, gasworks, chapels of worship and even new brickyards which soon found themselves working flat out to keep up with demand for bricks!

However, in recent times the Leen Valley - rather like the rest of the country - has again undergone dramatic change. The industrial revolution era has gone to be replaced by the age of new technology. Major industries have either vanished entirely or else have dramatically contracted in the post-Second World War years. In the Leen Valley district, once a roaring furnace of industry, the fires have died. Gone are the coalmines and virtually all the railways that once served them. Ironworks, brickyards and coke ovens are history and gas-making has vanished along with the brewing of beer while bleaching and dyeing are no longer the major industries they once were.

Happily some world-class industries that made the valley their home have survived in the new age. Rolls Royce still develop and test aero engines at Hucknall and Raleigh bicycles are still built at Radford.

What happened to the district in the late twentieth century is a microcosm of what happened to Great Britain. There has been a move away from the once labour-intensive mass employers like coal-mining to much smaller and cleaner concerns and there is no better illustration of this than at Bulwell where the former colliery site is now occupied by a factory making home improvement products.

Touring the district now, it is hard to believe that so much industry and activity, much of it now vanished, came about in such a compact corner of Nottinghamshire.

Although this work is far from comprehensive the intention here is to give the reader a glimpse into how it used to be and what made the Leen Valley 'tick'. For in the two centuries under review, this small sector of former countryside developed an industrial base unique in the East Midlands.

Martin Weiss

THE LEEN VALLEY MILLS

FOREST ROAD leaves the main A60 exactly halfway between Nottingham and Mansfield . . . half a mile north of the Seven Mile House. Take the left turn and you'll soon be in the picturesque village of Papplewick which, to the casual passer-by, appears to consist of a few cottages and other dwellings flung out from a busy crossroads dominated by a garage and filling station on one corner and the village pub on the other.

By following Forest Road the traveller will descend steadily down the shallow eastern flank of the upper Leen Valley. A vista opens out revealing, on the horizon, the wooded hills of Annesley Park more or less straight ahead. Down on the valley bottom and in the middle distance can be seen, on a sunny day, the church tower of St Michael's, Linby. Moving a little to the left and the sprawl of Hucknall and Butler's Hill comes into view with the skyline here dominated by the soaring chimney stacks of the former Watnall brickyard across on the opposite ridge.

In short it is a pastoral panorama with little to suggest there might have been any heavy industrial activity in the recent past. But this impression is quite misleading for if we were able to turn back the clock half a century and look again we should soon spot the smouldering spoil heaps in the middle distance giving away the locations of coalmines; we would also spy out trails of smoke and steam marking the progress of an assortment of trains while everywhere would be a smoke haze from hundreds of domestic hearths.

None of this however quite encroached upon Papplewick though it was a near miss!

A quirk of fate, in this case the growth of the Lancashire cotton-spinning industry, led to the relatively swift demise of the Leen Valley cotton mills within the first two decades of the nineteenth century. For in or around the year 1800 Papplewick was THE industrial centre of the Leen Valley. What's more it was the cradle of steam power. Two of the six big cotton mills on the River Leen at the time were, it is believed, the pioneers of rotary steam power in the cotton spinning industry. But in spite of the village's claim to fame as a shrine to the industrial revolution Papplewick has, over the years seemingly never wanted to make much fuss about its heritage.

For example of the six mills that were erected and operated by the

Robinson family in the upper Leen Valley only three have survived. Of the three only one is a well-known landmark today and, once again, it was a near miss. The prominent Castle Mill just outside Papplewick on the way to Linby was very nearly demolished soon after the end of the Second World War and a writer in the *Nottingham Journal* for 19 July, 1946, warned 'Castle Mill is doomed to destruction with very little chance of reprieve in spite of strenuous efforts by local authorities. This pseudo-Gothic mill, built around 1777, now stands in a state of peaceful decay but unless there is an unexpected last-minute reprieve its ancient stonework will be pulverized into road-making rubble.'

Luckily for posterity, it was saved and not only that, went on to benefit from a full restoration which created two penthouse-style apartments. In the process the builder who carried out the work won himself an award.

Perhaps at the time when the old buildings were under threat Papplewick had a pang of regret at the prospect of losing touch with the last big monument to its industrialized past. At any rate the local parish council of the day fought hard to keep the mill.

The report went on: 'The Mill and Dam are both the property of the Hucknall Torkard Industrial Provident Society Limited who have ordered the demolition and drainage (of the dam). The owners' opinion, stated by Mr G.H. Green, manager of the society, is that

Fishing in Papplewick Dam circa 1925
Photo: Nottinghamshire County Council Leisure Services

there is no question of destroying a local amenity. Rather, he suggests, is the society doing a public service for it will make nothing out of the demolition and the society's action will allow for a road improvement.

'The property belongs to our members,' he says 'and they can do what they like with it. I don't believe that 90 per cent of them care whether the Mill or Dam are there or not.'

However Papplewick and Linby Parish Council weighed in to support the 'Save our Mill' campaign and the Rector of Linby, the Rev L.I. Butler, joined the growing chorus of protest which was sparked off when the owners started to drain the large dam across the road from the mill. Within a few days the water level in the dam had dropped noticeably and thousands of fish were netted and transferred to other homes including Wollaton Park and the River Trent.

So the story ended happily for Castle Mill although, of course, the Hucknall Torkard Industrial

Castle Mill, rear elevation, prior to restoration circa. 1946 with waterwheel in situ.
Photo: John Archer

Provident Society Limited did achieve part of their plan with their successful draining of the dam which in turn enabled that intended road improvement to be carried out. When one considers the volume of heavy vehicles now using the road passing Castle Mill it was inevitable that, sooner or later, some improvements would have been necessary to cope with 20th century traffic.

Present day traffic - and this road was infested with an endless procession of lorries prior to a weight restriction order coming into operation - would be hard pressed to cope with the 1946 alignment which wound sharply around the front of the mill buildings. The original road is now the owners' access and parking space!

Castle Mill variously also known as Linby Mill or even Upper Mill occupied the site of an earlier corn mill which was mentioned in the Domesday Book. Furthermore, and long before the entrepreneurial Robinson era, the River Leen is said to have powered no fewer than twenty mills between Newstead and Lenton making it, by all accounts, one of the busiest milling rivers in the kingdom.

In a paper written for The Thoroton Society in the summer of 1916 Mr Harry Gill noted that the Robin Hood Hills run east and west across the Forest of Kirkby and form a watershed for two important tributaries of the Trent.

The Erewash issues on the north side flows westwards for some distance until it reaches Pinxton and thence it becomes the western boundary of the county and flows southwards to the Trent, while a number of springs which issue on the south side, when joined to the waters from Hollin Well, flow in a meandering course almost due south. This watercourse is now known as the River Leen, a corruption through various renderings of the Celtic word Llyn for lake or pool and 'hylynna' meaning streamlet.

Mr Gill added: 'The ancient names were descriptive and accurate for the distance from source to confluence is not more than ten miles as the crow flies. Perhaps no other stream of equal size attracted so

Castle Mill circa 1925, front elevation showing the original course of the main road which is now a residents' car park

Photo: Nottinghamshire County Council Leisure Services

much attention as did the Leen in medieval days. It formed the western boundary of the King's great Forest of Nottingham (or 'Shirewood') and it fed the fish stews and supplied the domestic needs of two important monasteries and a Royal Castle, while on its banks stood a succession of mills at one time numbering more than a score; for although the fall of the valley is but gentle the volume of the flow is sufficient to turn a 'breast wheel' or an 'undershot' mill wheel at very frequent intervals throughout its course.'

Even in the 18th century a description of the route taken by the Leen rings familiar for it was said that one mile from its source the stream entered the Augustinian Priory at Newstead and then flowed down to Papplewick (on the left bank) and Linby (Leen-by) on the right reaching the ancient Forge Mill about midway between Hucknall and Bulwell when it becomes the northern boundary of the extended city of Nottingham.

'Thus far the river valley is verdant with meadows and woodlands as of yore. The lower half of the course now skirts the ragged edges of the city, and for years past the stream has been polluted and befouled with refuse from numerous bleach yards and dye works. . . The waters of the River Leen were always attributed with properties making them especially suitable for such industries as bleaching and dyeing but as these water-side industries grew so did the pollution and in his 1983 book *The Leen Valley* Claude Bartholomew states that the reputation of some local family-run businesses mainly in Bulwell and Basford became household words throughout the textile industry 'but with the great increase of factories and other industries along the Leen Valley the River Leen, which had been a very good source of drinking water, rapidly became nothing more than an open sewer by the time it reached the Trent at Nottingham.'

It was to Bulwell that the ambitious George Robertson came in about 1737. He left his Scottish home but, it is said, quickly changed his name to Robinson since Scottish people were not popular south of the border at this period. He may have become George Robinson on paper, so to speak, but no one has yet explained how he managed to disguise a Scottish accent!

Unpopular or otherwise there is no doubt that George Robinson was a most accomplished businessman, perhaps one of Nottinghamshire's most astute and talented men of commerce of all time. . . for by the end of his working days he had built up a veritable empire along the banks of the River Leen which he presided over with his sons during the latter years of the 18th century. He died in 1798 and is buried at Bulwell. The business which he started carried on into the early decades of the 19th century by which time cotton spinning was being centralized in Lancashire.

But with the far-sightedness and business acumen typical of the Robinsons they had identified the trend in plenty of time and moved on to pastures new. The mill buildings were either leased or sold for other uses while the family concentrated their talents and assets on a successful banking venture.

Another Leen Valley writer, J.D. Marshall, took a particular interest in the activities of the Robinsons and he, in turn, drew upon the studies of an even earlier chronicler, Alderman Robert Mellors, who revealed that by 1776 the Walk or Warp Mill at Papplewick was complete and with a sizable dam parallel to the present Moor Road. (It is the remains of this dam, it is thought, which can still be found within Moor Pond Wood though the area is now a nature reserve with properly laid out footpaths).

Alderman Mellors drew attention to the Chapman Survey of that year since on it were marked all water mills then working on the Leen . . . and there was no mention of Castle, Grange, Middle or Forge mills. The writer believed they were not built until the following year.

Mr Marshall said: 'They were almost certainly not built at the time of the survey. Nor is there any reason to expect a very rapid progression of the industry before the late seventies when Arkwright's already established factories at Cromford and Nottingham could have been expected to stimulate emulation. In 1780 one or more of the Papplewick mills certainly existed (ie. in addition to the Walk/Warp Mill) for the owners were advertising in the *Nottingham Journal* for blacksmiths and it was said perhaps significantly that 'if men with families, they will likewise have work and good wages'. In 1782 the same newspaper reported that a man had been drowned in the dam belonging to the Papplewick cotton mills 'where he had been with a load of lime,' suggestive that building work was in progress.'

By about 1785 the sizable Grange Mill a few hundred yards below the Warp Mill had been built and in the following year a reviewer noted that Messrs Robinson owned 'several large and valuable cotton works' in the vicinity.

By the time the family's cotton mills were all coming on stream (to use an appropriate phrase) the founder, George Robinson, was probably too elderly or infirm to manage all the works himself and the main day-to-day responsibility was taken by sons John and James Robinson, the latter conducting correspondence on behalf of his father. It appears that the Robinsons approached Messrs Boulton and Watt about the purchase of a steam engine some time in 1784; the arrangements to transport a boiler and castings from Birmingham via Derby to Papplewick had already been made by January 1785.

Bulwell was the dividing point between the upper Leen and its mills and the lower Leen bleaching and dyeing industries. Joseph Robinson (George Robinson's second son) remained in the latter business while John and James Robinson were busy developing the cotton mills. The cotton produced in the mills went downstream to be bleached and dyed by the same family.

We'll take a closer look at the mills and their early application of steam power shortly. First, though, a reminder that it wasn't technological innovation for which they are best remembered . . . rather for the sad stories of child labour.

In the public perception mills have never been noted as ideal places of travail and many have been the stories of young children being worked long hours by cruel masters. The modern idea of life working in a mill (any mill anywhere at this period) revolves around the concept of near slavery.

For generations after their demise, stories were told of the sad lot of youngsters who worked and allegedly died of overwork and malnutrition. Until recent times, nobody had ever really studied the facts giving rise to these tales which, over the years, have been absorbed into local folklore.

In the autumn of 1986, however, the Association for Industrial Archaeology published *The Robinson Enterprises at Papplewick* to

Warp Mill, Papplewick, returned to residential use.
Photo: Nottinghamshire County Council Leisure Services

coincide with the bi-centenary of the installation of the first steam rotary engine to drive cotton spinning machinery by the Robinsons at Papplewick on the River Leen. Author Nan Greatrex applied herself to producing, as far as records would allow, the most comprehensive study of the subject so far attempted.

Discussing working conditions in the mill (of which more later) the author writes: 'The early mill owners have been branded as hard and greedy men who treated their workers, and most especially their child workers, very harshly. The Robinsons have suffered such allegations, which seem to have been based on the burial record for Linby parish church which shows between 1799 and 1814 the names of forty-two boys, each called a 'London boy' or 'an apprentice of Mr Robinson'.

'No cause of death is suggested although one boy drowned while swimming in the mill dam. However a Professor J.D. Chambers has commented that this was a notorious period of famine and fever with a raging epidemic of smallpox, and deaths for the whole area were high. He also noted that these deaths did not occur until almost fifteen years after the mills came into existence.'

Nan Greatrex goes on: 'In the meantime legend has taken over and the forty-two deaths of apprentice boys has increased almost fourfold to a reputed 163. The basis for this seems to be an article on churches in the *Mansfield Reporter* in 1907 in which the author had been curious about the "London boys" in the parish register'.

Part of this article is quoted and the writer identifies the spot where the bones of the unfortunate youths are laid adding that the contemporary belief was that the boys whether 42 or 160 were poorly fed causing some of the weaker ones to die, quite literally, of malnutrition.

The revised figure of 160 seems to have been attributed to Reverend Weddell who became Rector of Linby in 1876 or 100 years after the mills were first built and his information was, therefore, heresay of over half a century later.

Nan Greatrex continues: 'The records of the magistrate, who dealt with absconding apprentices in the area, show that there were fewer cases (presumably of smallpox) than in comparable establishments.

'So were the Robinsons bad masters, or have they been maligned down the years?'

The author's researches would seem to suggest that far from being 'sweat shops' and giving rise to working conditions leading to the deaths of young children, the Robinsons' mills were quite properly run to the satisfaction of not only the owners, but also at least to some of the workers, not to mention government agents.

For example, she draws upon a report on working conditions given before the Select Committee on the *State of Children employed in Manufactories*, in 1816, which showed that in the general respect of working hours the Robinson mills were similar to other large and well-run establishments. Also, part of a report by an inspecting magistrate and clergyman, declared the premises to be 'comfortable in all seasons, with employees working twelve hours daily starting at six in the morning and ending at seven in the evening with sufficient time allowed for three meals within that period'.

And the report added that child apprentices were well-clothed, smart and cheerful and gave the impression of being quite happy with their lot. And, to boot, their standard of education was 'far beyond what could have been expected of children in their situation.'

In summing up, the report went on to say: 'The establishment appears to us conducted with the utmost propriety and humanity'.

The Robinsons, it would appear, attached great importance to giving children within their employment a good start in life and in this respect schooling was keenly promoted to the extent that the Robinsons were prepared to subsidize the cost of education where necessary.

A member of the Robinson family maintained that after leaving the mills the young adults became good soldiers and sailors and good farmers' servants and in other various capacities. Some local schools were actually funded by the family as was the custom among some millowners at that period.

Two female employees who had worked in the Leen Valley mills between 1798 and 1814 gave evidence in 1833 before the Commissioners into the Employment of Children in Factories.

A Mrs Fortescue and a Mrs Marsden both gave accounts of their working careers in the mills and declared themselves to be fit and healthy despite their years of twelve hour days. Mrs Fortescue's only complaint was about the cotton flues flying about in the air which invariably ended up in her food. Mrs Marsden went to work in the mills at six years old and 'staid' until she was seventeen and thought she had not suffered any ailment in consequence.

Their respective accounts were given some years after the closure of the Papplewick mills so even if they had chosen to be critical of their former workplace there was unlikely to be any repurcussion. In short, if conditions at Papplewick were as bad as the Rector claimed, then there was certainly no hint of it in the statements of those who actually worked there. One account however, does mention a waiting list of potential employees.

Sad though the deaths of the children were it does not follow, however, that they died as a direct result of being overworked and undernourished by their employers, in which case it is open to historical speculation as to why the stories about the children began to circulate after half a century.

It certainly seems odd that an enterprise that was so enlightened in its approach to new technology as to be among the first to install rotary steam power, should want to more or less kill off the potential cream of its future workforce by working them to death.

Stanley D. Chapman in his 1967 work *'The Early Factory Masters'* agrees that children from London came to Nottinghamshire to work in cotton mills although he does not specifically identify the Robinson sites but does mention others elsewhere within the county. He offers no evidence of such children being maltreated by employers but suggests some may have arrived in poor health arising from their upbringings in the capital rather than because of any shortcomings in the condition of their employment.

If a person were still to believe in the theory that the children were victims of 'exploitation', then they could consider why this 'exploitation' was only countenanced after fifteen years of the mills being in operation. Or was there simply a lingering bad feeling in some quarters towards the Robinson family even long after their mills had closed. A bad feeling, moreover, that manifested itself in unpleasant rumours.

Whatever the answers we can be sure of one fact: the Leen Valley mills were not destined to last . . . in fact their demise was surprisingly swift. The Robinson venture ended with them operating at six separate sites in the valley, but by 1820 the family had withdrawn from cotton spinning and gone into banking instead.

The mills carried on for a time after the Robinson family had relinquished their interest until the early 1830s. But after that date cotton spinning ended. Technology which gave the mills a head start in the late 18th century had overtaken the venture by the first half of the 19th and cotton spinning retreated to Lancashire.

So by 1850 the once-busy Papplewick area was, according to a guidebook, 'once the seat of an extensive cotton manufactory of which James Robinson Esq. was the proprietor; the deserted mills and once-thronged cottages of the work people are still standing in all their loneliness and for the most part hastening to decay'.

Maps of Papplewick and Linby dating from 1847 show a complex network of river, water channels, ponds and canals on which the Leen Valley cotton mills depended for their motive power. But with a river as small as the Leen the Robinsons would have been very vulnerable to any interruption in water supply . . . in fact no sooner was Forge Mill finished than, as James Robinson, the founder's son, later wrote, 'Lord Byron put us to much expence'.

The fifth Lord Byron, great uncle of the poet, lived at Newstead Abbey just north of Papplewick, and according to stories of the time was a very unpopular and mischievous character who was in financial dire straits himself and was envious of the apparent success of the Robinsons' cotton milling enterprise.

Although the success or otherwise of the mills was beyond the landowner's control he did have ultimate power over the water which drove the machinery within the mills . . . and he was determined to cause trouble.

Since the Leen had its source on the Newstead estate Lord Byron decided to restrict the flow of water by damming it up on his property and denying the Robinsons their vital source of power, an act which not only threatened the mill-owners but their workers too. So with their whole enterprise at risk the elderly George Robinson went to London to seek an injunction to restrain Lord Byron.

The penniless Newstead aristocrat had explained to him how the Robinsons were suffering great financial loss as a result of his actions but he still refused to co-operate. In a fit of pique he 'pulled the plug' quite literally on the millions of gallons of impounded water held in his lakes at Newstead, and caused a great flood of water to be

Forge Mill at Bestwood was reduced from six to three sotreys after a fire.
Photo: Nottinghamshire County Council Leisure Services

released down the upper Leen Valley. What effect this onrush had elsewhere along the valley is not recorded, but only the quick action of employees at Castle Mill saved it from serious damage, as the dam there rapidly filled as a result of the sudden deluge.

In the end the Robinsons won the day and the legal process eventually found against Lord Byron and his anti-social behaviour. It appears that Lord Byron, while restrained, was still simmering and he had no intention of giving in easily. He made it clear he intended to pursue the battle to win 'his' water rights, though it will probably remain one of the mysteries of history how he expected to pay for litigation.

The Robinsons, for their part, had so much at stake that they could not afford the time or money to engage in long drawn out legal disputes. They had already been losing £500 per week, thanks to Lord Byron's policy of starving them of water, and the prospect of ongoing aggravation did not appeal.

Steam power was still in its infancy at this period . . . but the Robinsons were increasingly desperate to find a solution to the dilemma and the question had to be asked: 'Was there any other form of motive power available which could be installed and set to work within a reasonable period of time?'

The answer did, indeed, appear to lie in the hands of Messrs Boulton and Watt of Birmingham and, as we have already seen, the feasibility of such an installation was being investigated in 1784. Parts began arriving the following year. But it must be remembered that the use of steam engines in industry was virtually unknown at this early period and, needless to say, there were teething problems which involved the younger generation of Robinsons in extensive correspondence with the makers.

The Summer of 1785 saw the Robinsons not only busy running their newly-commissioned mills but now also wrestling with the extra management responsibility of dealing with the introduction of, to them, new technology. Boulton and Watt were obviously aware that if their engine was to prove satisfactory, further orders might be forthcoming for the other mills under the Robinsons' control.

At this time the Robinsons were engaged in the building of their fifth mill and the design of this building already allowed for the installation of a steam engine.

Historians who take an interest in Leen Valley matters cannot be certain in which of the mills the Boulton and Watt engine was first tried, but some agree upon the long-vanished Lower Mill where old records have revealed an insurance policy being in force. The steam engine there was said to be insured for £400.

Evidence does exist that a second Boulton and Watt rotary engine was installed at the Robinsons' Old (Grange) Mill and was working by 1790. At any rate, and even though this all happened long before the days of smoke control orders, James Robinson wrote to Boulton and Watt during 1791 complaining about smoke nuisance.

The upshot of this was a letter from the company saying: 'We can safely say that our engines at this manufactors are absolutely without smoke except a little at first lighting the fires, and sometimes on throwing on fresh coal when the fire has been suffered to fall too low, which may be avoided. When it does smoke it is always the fault of the engine man'.

Steam power never fully took over from water; millworkers themselves preferred the steady flow of power generated by the water wheel to the somewhat jerky progress of those early steam engines. Also during the period 1785-90 litigation dragged on over the Lord Byron business; he who had been the cause of the sudden need to find alternative means of powering the mill machinery. In the end the mill-owners triumphed over the tetchy aristocrat at Newstead and the record tells of no further episodes of the River Leen being dammed up or of sudden inundations. But during all this, those early steam engines were not necessarily trouble free.

Landowners upon whose estates the mills had been built appear to have been uneasy about the sudden influx of labour. This was particularly so at Papplewick where a town of considerable size was becoming established. We have already seen how Lord Byron addressed the problem of having a small industrial town materialize just down the road from his stately isolation at Newstead. But there is no evidence of Lord Montagu of Papplewick Hall resorting to such drastic measures. One has to assume that he took a more liberal stance. Certainly, the Robinsons would have numbered among the local gentry, albeit in the lower ranks as such. A mere cotton spinner, wealthy though he might be, did not intermingle with Byrons, Chaworths or Montagus except on formal occasions. No doubt the local aristocracy were not unduly upset when cotton milling came to a premature end in the vicinity.

In early 1831 all the mill machinery was auctioned and in 1834 some of the larger fixed assets were offered for sale. Eventually the Robinsons left Papplewick Grange, which had been the family home, and re-established themselves south of the Trent at Widmerpool, where they remained until the 1920s.

Once cotton spinning had ceased the landowners in Papplewick

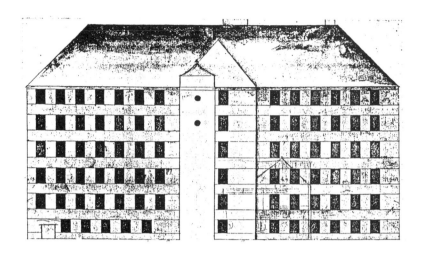

The 'monstrous' six storey Lower Mill, would have been a skyscaper by 18th Century standards . It was demolished in the mid 19th Century.

and Linby moved to 'encourage' former millworkers to move out of the immediate district to places like Hucknall and Bulwell. They were determined to keep the two villages free of industry. To underline that fact they arranged for most of the workers' former houses to be demolished. The demise of three of the original mill buildings was

Clerk's House, Bestwood, a scaled down version of Lower Mill?

Photo: Author

probably also attributed to this policy of de-industrializaion. The three surviving mills no doubt escaped because they were, initially, converted back to corn mills and were therefore, not labour intensive in the same way as a cotton mill.

To those who had an interest in preserving the rural environment and the appearance of the upper Leen Valley, the monstrous Lower Mill (somewhere midway between Grange Mill and Forge Mill) must have been an awesome spectacle. That six-storey giant towering over the landscape would have been a veritable skyscraper. A surviving drawing of the building gives the impression of a gaunt, prison-like structure, quite different from the relatively rustic appearance of Castle Mill.

There is at Bestwood a three-storey house still standing at the side of the footpath leading to Hucknall, which was once part of the Lower Mill complex of buildings. It is worth studying since it is an impressive structure that gives some idea, in scaled down form, of how the main building might have looked.

RAILS IN THE LEEN VALLEY

IF WE ACCEPT the generally held view that the 'golden age' of steam railways in this country was during the 1930s then it could be said that steam's 'Indian Summer' came two decades later in the 1950s . . . so let's go back to one of the Leen Valley's most picturesque villages and relive a weekday late summer evening while we watch the trains go by.

Mid-1950s Linby then, as now, remains an unspoilt rural Nottinghamshire village with rustic cottages, farm buildings hiding not far away behind the trees, a couple of weathered stone crosses at either end of the main street, a quaint old school, Post Office and pub while half of the main thoroughfare is flanked by streams running in shallow gullies and neatly fenced - the famous Linby 'Docks'.

As we walk up the street towards St. Michael's Church we find it hard to imagine that here we are in one of the upper Leen Valley's busiest railway locations, not to mention the fact that the village has lent its name to one of the district's most productive coalmines . . .

A gloomy scene at Radford Station as a Nottingham to Worksop local restarts for its journey north through the Leen Valley towards Mansfield - next stop Basford Vernon. The pointwork in the foreground is where the line splits to Trowell and the Erewash Valley. Photo: D. Swale

for within the village itself there is no sign of a train or even a cobble of coal.

Linby has escaped the despoliation of the industrial revolution, but only just. The pit and the railways may not be visible from the front door of the Horse and Groom, but there's no escaping the sounds that are a permanent workaday background to mid-1950s Linby.

Passing the church on our left we climb a short rise leading up to the bridge carrying Wighay Road out of the village and over the Great Northern line; the former stationmaster's house can be seen across the road.

Not far away comes the sharp 'bark' of a steam winding engine striking up. The beat is slow at first but gathers momentum and then dies away. After a pause the sound repeats itself. First come a few sharp blasts, quickening as we listen . . . then the sound fades away once again.

To Linby locals the sound of the steam engine drawing coal goes unnoticed. Although barely half a mile away the coalmine makes no other intrusion on the village. Indeed most of the workforce live in or around Hucknall. Linby never became a pit village and escaped having rows of colliers' terraces thrust upon it in the 19th century.

As we breast the top of the bridge, however, the surface buildings of Linby Colliery can be clearly seen over to our left . . . headstocks, coal preparation plant, washery, railway sidings and much else presided over by a tall chimneystack. Steam spurts up suddenly from a building beneath the headstocks and, again, the winder gathers momentum while the wheels atop the headstocks flicker around. Further across our field of vision lies the sprawling spoil tip, parts of which are smouldering and giving forth acrid, sulphurous fumes.

The entire spoil tip is surmounted by an aerial ropeway which draws a revolving procession of 'tip and skip' tubs up to the summit where, at a fixed point, each tub overturns and pours its load of waste down.

Ahead of us Wighay Road curves down to the level crossing where the Midland Railway lines from Nottingham to Mansfield cross and, just a few hundred yards further on, another bridge can be seen carrying the Great Central line from Nottingham Victoria to Sheffield. The embankment runs along to our right hand side.

From our rear comes the 'whine' of a lorry engine and shortly we are passed by a red 'Tomlinson' Bedford which drops away and rattles over the level crossing. And as the sound recedes we are rewarded by the approaching sound of our first train. Up on the

Great Central 'down' main line a smartly turned-out mixed traffic B1 class engine is lifting the London Marylebone to Bradford (Forster Square) return express. 'The South Yorkshireman' is running to time and looks to be in fine fettle as its crew, up on the footplate, work their locomotive speedily up the rising gradient towards Annesley. Behind the engine is an impressive train of red and cream coaches including a restaurant car.

Quite a few businessfolk will be rounding off their evening meals and perhaps glancing out of their carriage windows, idly studying the mixed landscape of fields, railways, farms and pits as wisps of smoke and steam drift back alongside the train.

We view 'The South Yorkshireman' as it begins to follow the curvature of the track away to the north after first crossing the decking over the Midland Railway line and shortly afterwards the substantial lattice girder span over the adjacent Great Northern route. The number on the engine cabside is a little indistinct, but there's no mistaking the fireman busy with his shovel for the driver will need a ready head of steam at his disposal all the way to Holmewood signal box near Chesterfield. For only here will he be able to ease back the regulator for the run down through Staveley Central.

The rhythmic sound of the engine's exhaust beat can be heard long after the train has been lost to view, but next our attention is quickly drawn to the level crossing and signal box just ahead. The signalman has already been busy operating the wheel which causes the crossing gates to swing shut across the road. From our right a Class 8F goods engine is drifting into view and very soon the Kirkby-in-Ashfield to Beeston marshalling yards coal train is passing through with the crew leaning out of the cabside to catch some welcome cool breeze, for conditions on this footplate are very hot and clammy. The clatter of some forty mineral wagons drowns out for a while the buzz of activity at Linby Colliery.

Also the passage of the Beeston-bound train has camouflaged the approach, down the Great Northern line, of the DIDO workmen's train consisting of a couple of drab non-corridor coaches which have arrived on the scene almost unnoticed.

We've been so busy admiring the passing of 'The South Yorkshireman' and studying the goods train on the Midland line that the DIDO crept up propelling its coaches from Newstead Station to Bulwell Common. It's one of those 'round-the-clock' workings that runs day in and day out taking crews on or off duty. In the end crews abbreviated the phrase day in, day out to DIDO!

As the DIDO passes almost beneath our feet we can lean over the bridge parapet and note the engine number 69692, an 0-6-2 side tank engine originally built for the Great Eastern Railway and later classified as N7 by the LNER after grouping in the early twenties. The DIDO has, over the years, become an institution in the Leen Valley scheme of things and is recognized instantly by folk in the valley towns with a certain degree of affection. It came into being as a result of the remote location of Annesley shed and yards and the consequent need to transport railway workers back and forth from the Hucknall, Bestwood and Bulwell areas.

The familiar aroma of steam and smoke is left lingering around the bridge as the DIDO rattles away towards Hucknall Town station.

Although it's a pleasant evening there comes one of those gentle summer showers. We hasten down to the level crossing gates and then turn sharp right on to the Linby southbound platform. A glance south down the 1 in 75 gradient towards Hucknall Colliery reveals a cloud of smoke billowing beneath the bridge at Byron station and up in the signal box there's a tinkle of bell codes as the Linby signalman prepares to 'accept' another train into his section of track from Nottingham.

The light shower persists as we await events on the platform and

A typical scene at Linby in the early 1960's as seen from the Nottingham platform of the village station. The train in the foreground, hauled by a Class 4F locomotive from Nottingham depot, is the Linby Colliery empties. The engine will have to pass beneath the Great Central deck and then some distance beyond before all its wagons are clear of the pointwork allowing reversal into the pit's reception sidings to take place. At this period, about 1963, both the Midland and Great Central lines remained very busy indeed and the frequency of freight trains along the Great Central was remarkable. In the centre of this picture is the unmistakable outline of an Annesley-based Standard Class 9F 2-10-0 which can be seen passing over the Midland. Although the locomotive appears to be running 'light' it was in fact hauling a mixed freight comprising some bogie flat wagons behind the tender. Photo: Author

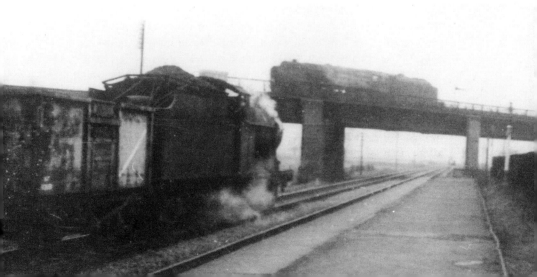

as the train slowly approaches, the gates once more swing shut across the road. The beat of the slow-moving locomotive dragging its wagons alongside Linby Colliery grows louder and more laboured.

Finally the engine, a Fowler Class 4F 0-6-0 goods, draws onto the crossing and, as it does so, the engine's driving wheels give a sudden and unexpected 'slip' causing the wheels to revolve involuntarily for a couple of seconds before grip is regained. This is caused by the locomotive 'tyres' losing adhesion on the brief stretch of rail already 'polished' by wet vehicle tyres.

By now the 4F is abreast our vantage point on the platform and we can study the inside cylinder motion through the solid steel frames as this tough old machine blasts past only a few feet away, its weight causing rail joints to dip as its six-coupled wheels pass over them.

The Linby Colliery empties has arrived.

The engine hauls its wagons on up the incline and soon passes beneath the Great Central deck just beyond the north end of the Nottingham platform where it finally comes to a stand. The train is, of course, still blocking the road at the level crossing and the few drivers who have been 'caught' decide to switch off their engines, sensing delay!

After the signal has 'cleared' to allow the brake van to cross over on to the 'up' line the guard detaches his van from the rear of the empties train, releases his brake and rolls backwards, through the points onto the 'up'.

Gravity is all that is needed in this part of the operation for the gradient falls away. As the van rolls over the pointwork its wheels bind. The guard allows the van to roll back a further few yards in order to keep a required clearance in readiness for the empties being set back into the colliery reception sidings.

Meanwhile, up in the signal box, the signalman sees an increasing build up of vehicles and decides, while the crossing is clear, to allow waiting drivers a chance to get on their way before shunting is resumed and the road blocked again.

Briefly the gates swing open and there's a whirr of starter motors as a mixed bag of cars and lorries resume their journeys after a period of enforced trainspotting. Once this manoeuvre is completed back go the gates once more. The pedestrian-only wicket gates also have to be secured.

Nearly half a mile up the line in the Newstead direction the crew of the 4F, who have no doubt taken the opportunity to enjoy a quick 'lid' of tea and a cigarette, wait for the signal to set back. Once confirmed the driver gently eases the empties back into the colliery sidings, all movements from now on coming under the guard's control as per regulations.

Not all the empties can be placed in any single siding so the engine has to draw forward a second time before the guard can switch points to allow the balance of the wagons to be accommodated. As soon as the empties have been safely placed in the north end of Linby Colliery yard reception sidings the immediate work of the loco crew, guard and signalman is complete. All that remains is for the 4F to rejoin its brakevan on the 'up' line and move off.

By this time, however, our attention is drawn to the Great Central and the approach of an evening stopping train from Nottingham Victoria to Sheffield Victoria. The powerful exhaust beat from the black class D11 locomotive demonstrates that number 62662 'Prince of Wales' is handling its five coach train with ease and, if anything, is showing signs of accelerating as it crosses above us. The view of the D11 is something of a treat since it represents one of the few big Great Central passenger types still surviving.

And from the opposite direction another train drifts into view on its way south . . . this time another Great Central stalwart, a Robinson 2-8-0 goods of the 04 class, is hauling a mixed freight possibly bound for Banbury or Woodford. J.G. Robinson was the Locomotive Engineer for the Great Central Railway, and his designs were sometimes considered to be among the best of the period. His 2-8-0 heavy goods design was so successful that many were built for work in France during the First World War though small numbers ended up as far away as Australia!

Well over an hour has elapsed while we've been watching the trains go by at Linby so we decide reluctantly to retrace our steps down the platform and, turning left, walk onto the bridge over the Great Northern route, noting the pit ponies in the field to our left hemmed in by railway lines on three sides of their field!

A glance to the right reveals the shadows deepening over the Leen Valley and the lights at Linby Colliery are beginning to glow. Our final view this evening as we set off home back towards Linby village is of the DIDO running, engine first, back towards Newstead. It may have been an idle hour for us but the trains and the pits will continue to run around the clock . . . not just at Linby but throughout the valley.

The foregoing scene, or variations on the theme, could have been applied to almost any part of the Leen Valley. At Annesley, for example, it was no exaggeration to say that the head of the valley was a tangle of through lines and marshalling yards, sidings and spoil tips, headstocks and smoking chimneys, while further down the valley at Bestwood a similar maze of tracks proliferated that, today, can only be comprehended by studying a contemporary Ordnance Survey map!

But the railway age in the Leen Valley would never have burgeoned as it did without the impetus of that key commodity COAL. As in the neighbouring Erewash Valley coal played such a dramatically important role in the progress of the local economy that the subject easily warrants and gets a chapter to itself.

As far back as the year 1604 there existed, by all accounts, a very early horse-drawn tramway built to carry coal mined in the Wollaton area. Although, for obvious reasons, no pictorial evidence exists of this railway or tramway most historians are proud to accept the written evidence for it gives Nottinghamshire the prestige of having developed the very first 'train' in the world.

Another two centuries elapsed before any further railway development occurred in the area. This time it materialized in the form of another horse-drawn waggonway built to convey freight between the canal basin at Pinxton and Mansfield. Traces can still be seen in woodland near Kirkby-in-Ashfield and subsequently much of the route was opened out and utilized later by the Midland Railway.

One could go on and list other, similar, enterprises elsewhere in the region like the Little Eaton gangway near Derby or the Cromford and High Peak Railway but these lines, while fascinating to study, are outside the scope of the present work.

It would be exciting to discover evidence of a waggonway or tramroad in the Leen Valley itself. The problem we encounter in trying to justify such a notion is that at the period such routes were being developed there was no industry as such in the district apart from quarrying of stone at Bulwell and, of course, the Robinsons' cotton mills in the Papplewick area.

However this has not dissuaded one writer from claiming that there WAS once a horsedrawn waggonway running from the Selston area pits down through Annesley Park to carry fuel for the Papplewick mills. Details of this venture were given briefly in 1983 by a Mr John Saint who wrote an article about the Papplewick cotton mills for members of Kirkby & District Conservation Society.

He wrote: 'I have reason to think that coal came along an early waggonway through Annesley Park from Selston and Bagthorpe pits to provide fuel for the steam engines at Papplewick. Horse-drawn waggons ran along an engineered trackway constructed by filling in and making embankments. I understand that it was possible to walk along all the route until the 1930s. It can still be partly followed by walking the footpath from Felley Mill Farm along the wood side to the bridge where the motorway crosses the path. There it turned right coming out in Hucknall. Of course it may have had nothing to do with the mills but the market for coal must have been large enough to justify spending on the laying of the track. Can this be earlier than the Mansfield and Pinxton Railway?'

If such a waggonway ever did exist it is unlikely it would have been laid down solely to provide coal for the two steam engines at Papplewick. Eric Horriben in his 1973 book *Hucknall: Of Lowly Birth and Iron Fortune* says that in any case the Robinsons were supplied with coal from Bilborough though he points out that because of the high delivered cost of such fuel the steam engines were by no means in continuous use.

Maybe the answer lies in a passage from a book written by a former Annesley vicar, Canon Frank Lyons. In *Hills of Annesley* published (in the USA!) in 1988, he mentions a coal wharf having been established 'on the edge of the hills overlooking the Erewash valley to the west'. It appears that two brothers, named Gill, set up this enterprise which was designed to draw coal and stone up the hillside from a pit or pits down below.

The author states: 'At the bottom of the hill was an open pit mine. Small tubs of coal were drawn to the surface by a rope attached to a revolving drum at the mine entrance. The drum was turned by two horses which walked in a circle around it whenever there was coal to be brought up. The pit also produced limestone. By the wharf at the top of the hill was a (steam) donkey engine which operated a large wooden roller. Chains attached to this roller pulled the tubs of coal or limestone up the hill and at the same time lowered empties down the side of the hill and back to the mine entrance.'

The price of coal at the wharf was seven shillings and sixpence a ton, 37$\frac{1}{2}$p.

'It seems that boys were used to operate the machinery. One day when one of these lads was in charge, he saw something had gone wrong and stopped the engine while he walked down the hillside to investigate. He had thought a truck had come off the rails which guided them up the hill but the cause was very different. A little girl had been sent by her mother to fetch milk from a farm at the bottom of the hill. She had had the idea of climbing onto a truck and taking a ride up the hillside. She was wearing a shawl wrapped around her neck. The wind blew the end of the shawl into the wheel and she was wrenched off the truck and crushed to death.'

Canon Lyons states that this inclined plane system came into use in 1827 and survived until 1884. The exact location is not certain but the Gill brothers would, one assumes, have selected the most favourable gradient available to them when laying down the rails. Careful fieldwork could yet reveal the whereabouts of this venture.

Unfortunately Canon Lyons did not elaborate further on the system. By the time the line went out of use more conventional railways were already well established in the Leen Valley proper and such a Heath Robinson-type system would probably have just faded out of the public eye and eventually been forgotten altogether. If this is, in fact, part of the system alluded to by Mr Saint one must ask did the rails extend beyond the top of the incline and in the Hucknall direction? Certainly in 1827 there were no pits operating in the Upper Leen Valley and there may well have been a worthwhile market for Erewash Valley coal literally from just over the hill. However by 1827, when the line came into use, the Robinsons were just about wrapping up their operations at Papplewick . . . the line, or waggonway, would have arrived on the scene some forty-two years too late!

Of the route mentioned by Mr Saint, from Felley Mill Farm to the site of the present M1 and then turning right to Hucknall, one must ask how horses might have dragged waggon loads of coal over such hilly terrain. If we are to assume they did then it is possible the route down to Hucknall joined the old Hucknall to Mansfield road at some point and then ran along it or beside it. However this is pure conjecture. For the time being we will have to leave Mr Saint's fascinating waggonway story for further research.

It is necessary to move further south to discover firm evidence of early railways in the Leen Valley and by 1844 Thomas North's important and extensive new coalmine at Cinderhill was in operation. (The site is now occupied by the Phoenix Business Park on the A 610.) Mr North's colliery was the first of what might be termed the district's seriously engineered deep mines. Confusingly it was also referred to as Babbington Colliery pinching the name of another older and smaller enterprise that used to operate at Babbington village or High Holborn halfway over the fields towards Ilkeston.

At or around this date a network of private mineral railway lines was built centred on Cinderhill and, for our purposes, it is interesting to study the one laid down from Cinderhill, via Whitemoor to Radford where coal was loaded into waiting boats on the Nottingham Canal. To clarify the following contemporary newspaper report one has to assume that the railway journey described was along the complete length of railway from the original Babbington village, via the new Cinderhill colliery and then down to Radford.

According to the *Nottingham Journal* who chronicled an early

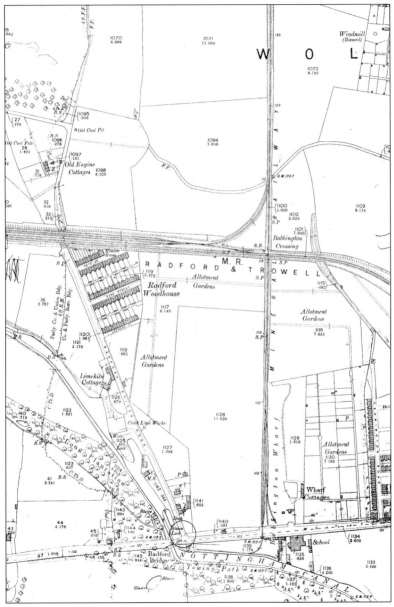

Nineteenth century Radford road, rail and canal topography. Thomas North's mineral railway runs (right) from top to bottom crossing the Radford to Trowell line of the Midland Railway. Radford Bridge Road allows us to pinpoint the present day 'Crown' traffic island on the Nottingham Ring Road system, see centre circle.

steam-hauled working in June 1838 a locomotive ran at 15 mph on a line operated by Messrs Wakefield & North at Cinderhill. By 1844 another publication the *Nottingham Review* recorded in considerable detail the VIP opening ceremony of the Cinderhill railway network and, unwittingly, almost certainly printed for posterity details of the first-ever passenger train working in the Leen Valley!

'The railway which has for so long a time been laid down by Messrs North, Wakefield & Co, from their offices at Cinderhill to the canal near Lord Middleton's park wall, and which has cost many thousand pounds is so far completed that coal is now conveyed thereupon every day, and put into the boats for water conveyance to different parts of the Kingdom. We learn that it was opened on Monday by the proprietors in the presence of a select party of their friends. About 12 o'clock the ladies and gentlemen comprising the party, about 17 in number, arrived at Babbington, a delightful spot seven miles from Nottingham, and having partaken of lunch, proceeded to view the apparatus used for the purpose of pumping water out of the pit, which is accomplished by three pumps sunk into a shaft 170 yards deep and worked by an engine of 120 horse power. Quitting the collieries, the next object of attraction was a beautiful chapel in the course of erection, for the purpose of enabling the inhabitants of the district, who are principally engaged in the collieries, to receive the benefits of religious instruction . . . At half past twelve o'clock the train was in readiness to convey the party along the line of railway and consisted of two carriages; the first tastefully decorated with flowers and evergreens, contained a lovely display of female beauty; the gentlemen occupied the second carriage, and on the signal being given the train started and was drawn by horse power for about half a mile after which it was attached to a rope and drawn up an inclined plane by a stationary engine. On being detached, for several miles it sped along through beautiful country, urged along by its impetus, down an inclined plane. About one o'clock it passed Basford, and in half an hour arrived at Radford Wharf, adjoining the canal, much to the surprise of many of the party, who little expected to find themselves so near Nottingham after having travelled about six miles on the newly formed railway. After waiting about twenty minutes the carriages were turned round, and shortly after two o'clock the party arrived at Cinderhill colliery.'

What a fascinating glimpse of an early railway excursion. The reader is left wondering at what stage of the journey the steam engine was employed. It seems odd that if the company owned a machine that could draw coal trains along at 15 mph (albeit six years earlier) they didn't want to show it off to their invited guests. Also the bit about the wagons being detached from the rope sounds a bit scary. One is left wondering how the wagons were controlled as they sped along downhill through the countryside! But it's all good stuff nevertheless and one can't help trying to visualize the pretty ladies and smartly-dressed gentlemen holding onto their hats while no doubt venturing a wave every now and again as their little train passed spectators gathered along the lineside.

The account appears in C.T. Goode's book *The Railways of Nottingham* and the author goes on to add: 'It must be remembered that the countryside was unspoiled and free of dense habitation at that time; the railway was only bothered by the crossing of various lanes: Bells, Broxtowe, Aspley and the Ilkeston Road. At the Radford end the railway met a short tramway running to the wharf from Radford Colliery. At Whitemoor, north of Radford, Thomas North opened his Newcastle Colliery in 1853, and from here he proposed further extensions, not put in hand, to Basford, Canning Circus, Trinity Square and Carrington, presumably for the distribution of coal. The Nottingham Mineral Railway, as the network was to be called, foundered on the expense of four tunnels totalling 1,706 yards and a 40ft. high viaduct.'

(The 'Radford Colliery' mentioned was presumably an earlier site than the later Wollaton/Radford combine mentioned elsewhere in this book.)

Part of this system the section between Bells Lane and the former coal wharf at the Newcastle Colliery site survived into relatively recent times. Extra-length level crossing gates were still in situ at the bottom of Bells Lane as late as the 1960s and the abutments of the over-bridge in Broxtowe Lane are still visible today although the latter was not part of the original formation. At the time of writing, part of this section of the old Nottingham Mineral Railway serves as a public footpath!

Mr Goode's research reveals that a twice-weekly National Coal Board train ran down from Cinderhill to the 'coal drops' at Whitemoor until 1966. He points out that the remains of the system towards Babbington vanished under the M1 and Nuthall by-pass developments.

Significant though it was in the build-up of the local railway system the comings and goings of coal trains on the Nottingham Mineral Railway to the west of the city were soon being eclipsed by more dramatic developments; for as early as 1839 the Midland Counties Railway which was quickly to emerge as the legendary Midland

Railway was operating steam-hauled trains between Nottingham and Derby . . . and within ten years the Midland had opened the first passenger-carrying line up the Leen Valley in 1848.

The term 'passenger carrying' is important here because it should be remembered that up to the year 1860 no coalmines existed in the upper Leen Valley. On the other hand the existence of rich coal reserves must have been clearly identified. It is hardly likely that one John Edward Ellis who went on to become one of the valley's leading coalmining entrepreneurs as well as being Chairman of the Midland Railway Board, would have put his money behind a line of railway JUST to carry passengers through obscure villages like Hucknall and Annesley.

When it was first proposed that a railway should be made from Nottingham to Mansfield and Worksop a certain witness, giving evidence before a Parliamentary committee, asked whether he was familiar with the country between Mansfield and Nottingham is reported to have replied: 'Perfectly. Do you imagine a railroad could be made from Mansfield to Nottingham? I should say it would not pay a farthing per cent.'

It is hard to believe that certain key people like Mr Ellis who were involved in the promotion of the line were unaware of the vast coal deposits potentially available right underneath the intended route.

Frederick S. Williams, in his magnificent tome *The Midland Railway: Its Rise and Progress* of 1876 writes: 'At that period, and for many years afterwards, it was not known how vast are the mineral resources of this valley. In 1868, however, Sir Roderick Murchison, who had more than once visited the Newstead and Hucknall districts, expressed the opinion: 'I believe that in all that country you will certainly find a very good coalfield; but these rich proprietors will never hear of having coalpits sunk near them.

'A very short time, however, had elapsed before the remunerative character of the coal trade improved; until, by the unprecedented increase of iron production, and the 'leaps and bounds' of manufacturing industry, the demand was so stimulated as to occasion the coal fever of 1872 and 1873, and landed proprietors here as elsewhere became anxious to lease their royalties. It may be safely said that there is no coalfield the possibilities of which are so large.'

Clearly, then, as now, everything has its price!

The landed gentry of Newstead, Papplewick, Bestwood and Bulwell, having become aware that they were literally sitting upon astronomical sums in royalties, can hardly be judged, retrospectively, to have been anything but human in their desires to make the most of a good thing . . . provided that the resulting despoliation was not visible from their own baronial bedchambers! This was proved to be exactly the case since none of the subsequent sinking sites was visible from the various halls and lodges involved.

Frederick S. Williams continues: 'The trains running from Nottingham to Worksop pass uninterruptedly over thirty miles of magnesian limestone and new red sandstone. The passenger looking eastward will see one after another costly and well-designed collieries rising, the shafts of which have recently penetrated the top hard coal at 400 yards or more from the surface. The royalties which have been let on the Nottingham and Mansfield line since the year 1870, now opening out, represent at least 500 million tons of coal.'

He went on to describe the route from Nottingham to Mansfield. 'We run for a short distance over the direct line to Trent, and then turn off to the north (Lenton South Junction, author). We have not gone far before we see on our left a new branch connecting this line with the Erewash via Radford, the new and extensive Wollaton Colliery, and Trowell, near Ilkeston. Wollaton Hall also is seen in the park upon the left (do remember, of course, that this area was still countryside at the time, author). Passing through busy mining and stocking-making populations, we reach Hucknall Torkard, in a vault within the church of which Byron was buried; and soon we are in the neighbourhood of Newstead, intimately associated with the memory of the poet. The Leen rises in the grounds of the Abbey. It is stated that a former owner of the estate received £10,000 special compensation for the injury inflicted upon it by the railway.' (Add some noughts to this figure to bring it up to late 20th century values, author.)

As first-comers along the valley the Midland Railway had one enormous advantage over later competitors in that they could pick the best route; or the line of least resistance from an engineering point of view. In reality the new line followed closely the course of the River Leen for most of its length, and at Basford and again at Bulwell, the rails crossed the water several times. By the time the railway reached the upper Leen Valley the river and the rails were some distance apart however.

There was nothing that might be termed a major engineering obstacle on the new railway until Robin Hood Hills were reached at Kirkby Forest and here a short tunnel pierced the hill at the very head of the valley and emerged into a deep sandstone cutting on the Nuncargate side of the high ground. This was originally known as the

Shoulder of Mutton tunnel and when navvies completed the bore in July 1848 they celebrated the occasion with a dinner at the Blue Bell Inn, Annesley Woodhouse.

(During 1994/5 the tunnel was re-excavated after having been infilled for some 20 years. It now enjoys a new lease of life as part of the Robin Hood route, author.)

On Monday September 23rd with track laid all the way from Lenton to Kirkby-in-Ashfield a small party of inspectors riding on two locomotives, one 30 tons and the other 36, made a trial run to test the line and two days later a government inspector gave the all clear for public services to begin. Notice was at once given that the line would be opened for passenger and goods traffic as far as Kirkby (the Kirkby to Mansfield section still being under construction) from Monday, 2 October, 1848.

The day of the line's opening also coincided with Nottingham's Goose Fair taking place and it was recorded that 'being fair week the number of travellers has been large' but cynics drew attention to the relatively high fares on the railway and prophesied that its popularity

The Midland Railway on its way from Nottingham to Mansfield relied heavily on level crossings wherever the line encountered a public highway. This was fine for the traffic of pre-motor age Nottingham but as the use of motor vehicles grew after the First World War, more and more of the original crossings had to be bridged to cope with 20th century traffic volumes. Here at Bobbers Mill the original level crossing is still in operation but a new bridge has appeared carrying the A610 Alfreton Road across the rails. Similar bridges were built over the railway to replace level crossings at Derby Road and Ilkeston Road. This view is probably from the 1930s and the chimney and headstocks of Radford Colliery are just visible behind the embankment which, by the looks of it, is still awaiting its fencing.
Photo: Nottingham Evening Post

would soon wear off. Nevertheless the Midland advertised three passenger trains each way every weekday and two each way on Sundays.

The Midland route from Kirkby onwards to Mansfield followed the sharply curved line of the old Mansfield & Pinxton Railway which had to be adapted to take the standard gauge track. This work was finally finished and the rest of the line opened to Mansfield on 9 October, 1849.

As well as the route from Radford to Trowell (on the Erewash Valley line) the Midland also pushed out another tentacle from their main line to Mansfield. This was the Basford to Bennerley Junction line which left the Mansfield line near Bulwell. It rose steadily upon an embankment eventually passing the western side of Bulwell before heading out towards Watnall where it entered a tunnel before emerging close to the Hardy & Hanson's Brewery at Kimberley continuing on to Bennerley near Ilkeston.

Travellers on the northbound M1 between Junctions 26 and 27 can still see one of the remaining bridges belonging to this line which stands, marooned, on the edge of a field with no trace of the railway to be seen!

When the M1 was being built through this area in the 1960s two other railway lines vanished under the tarmac. One was the Midland's branch up to Watnall Colliery which left the Basford to Bennerley line immediately after the bridge just mentioned. The other was the Barber, Walker company's mineral railway which started off at Langley Mill and threaded its way past pits at Moorgreen and High Park, meandered up Beauvale past the Priory and, after connecting with Watnall Colliery, went on to cross a bridge over the Midland line before terminating at a coal wharf near the former Blanchard's bakery. In the Leen Valley scheme of railway development neither of these routes was of great significance.

Anyone who is sufficiently interested can still see a trace of the old Midland formation near Watnall. Both the Midland and the Barber, Walker lines ran parallel and passed underneath Watnall Road not far from Watnall corner at EXACTLY the same spot as the present bridge over the M1! The old Midland line can be seen on the left-hand side between hedging striking out over the fields. The Barber, Walker formation is now the southbound fast lane of the motorway - how times change!

Mining operations spread northwards up the Leen Valley into the 1870s . . . and the Midland was well placed to service the fast-growing demand for coal haulage. At Hucknall, for example, when the rails were first laid down they passed what was then a fairly dingy little town populated by, for the most part, poor framework knitters. Within two or three decades, however, Hucknall had become a major new industrial town with two pits of its own, one in Portland Road and the other on Watnall Road, while nearby Linby Colliery was so close to Hucknall that it might just as well have been Hucknall No.3.

It was good news for the forward looking Midland Railway. In a nutshell they were enjoying a monopoly in moving Leen Valley coal from the pitheads to the marketplace . . . and doing very nicely in the process!

To re-cap, then, we have seen how the first railway line came to the Leen Valley and how it was an important spin-off from the pioneering Midland Counties Nottingham to Derby route. By following the general course of the river, engineers were able to build the line quickly and with no major natural obstacles to overcome, except for a tunnel leading the tracks beneath Robin Hood Hills. We have to bear in mind, however, that for most of its journey north to Kirkby-in-Ashfield and eventually Mansfield the line passed through a rural landscape unsullied by major industry. Passenger trains operated daily but, it was felt, would not offer serious competition to road-going passenger transport at least until the railway trimmed its fares.

However the Midland had bigger ideas for the railway. It certainly hadn't been built for the entertainment of the locals whatever they felt about ticket prices. Coal revenues were what counted and the Midland Railway's gamble in building their Nottingham to Mansfield route would pay handsome dividends.

But the rival Great Northern Railway were anxious for THEIR piece of the action in this very lucrative coalfield.

In their book *An Account of Railway Development in the Nottinghamshire Coalfield* published shortly after the end of the Second World War, John A. Birks and Peter Coxon note: 'By 1879 the G.N. had discovered that in assuming the Erewash Valley to be the source of the entire coal trade in the area they had been mistaken. Some years previously, the Midland Railway Company had realized the importance of the Leen Valley and had accordingly promoted branches to cater for it. Now their rival saw that the value of the coal traffic passing over those lines was almost the same as that over the Erewash lines, and, as it was entirely a Midland Company monopoly, decided to tap it as soon as possible.

'Accordingly, in the session of 1880, the G.N. directors promoted a Bill for a branch eight miles long from their existing line at Bulwell up the Leen Valley to Newstead to connect en-route with Bestwood

Never famous for exciting expresses, the former Great Northern company's Leen Valley extension line passed most of its life carrying an endless and monotonous procession of coal trains from the pits to Colwick Yards at Netherfield along with balancing empties workings. It is just such an empty wagon train that was pictured here shortly after joining the route near Leen Valley Jn. in 1960. The train is headed by a 2-8-0 'Austerity' of Colwick shed, an engine type that proliferated around Nottingham at this period. Its destination was probably Hucknall Colliery. The Great Central main line ran just behind the photographer on the opposite side of Hucknall Road. Note the former GNR lower quadrant (distant) signal.
Photo: C.A. Hill

and other important collieries. This was duly passed and, by 1881, the work on the line had commenced. By July coal trains were running from Bestwood Colliery and, on 18 October, mineral traffic began in earnest. Almost a year later on 2 October, 1882, the coalfield's development was approaching its zenith.'

Before we delve any further into developments it might be useful to pause and consider briefly the route taken by the G.N. metals. As often happens with railway lines so much of the infrastructure has been lost under modern development that the exact course is not easily traceable and will become even more obscure as years go by.

The Great Northern Railway already had what became locally known as its 'back line' running from Colwick out in a big semi-circle around the north of Nottingham. The line passed through Mapperley Tunnel before climbing to Daybrook, running along to Leen Valley Junction and then on to Basford North and out towards Derby via its appropriately named Derbyshire Extension.

The new line heading towards the Leen Valley pits left the so-called 'back line' at what is now the junction of Arnold Road and Hucknall Road where it ran alternately in cuttings and then upon embankments along the eastern flank of Bulwell Common before finally swinging away from the Bulwell/Basford area towards Bestwood. Later, after crossing both the River Leen AND the rival Midland Railway at Butler's Hill the G.N. ran directly into the western boundary of Hucknall Colliery yard, passed through Hucknall Town station and then crossed underneath the Midland again before reaching the sidings at Linby Colliery. After Linby the line ran north to Newstead, for much of the time in a shallow sandstone cutting so that an observer in the fields might only see the top half of any passing engine!

As second-comer in the Leen Valley the Great Northern had to select a more heavily-engineered route than the earlier Midland Railway. The G.N. tracks twisted around their rival's more or less straight line and the G.N. also had to fork out extra cash to build bridges and earthworks . . . something that the Midland had not had to bother with to any great extent.

Today the formation can still be partly followed in the Bulwell area and the section north of Linby now forms a footpath and nature trail. But in Hucknall almost all trace of the old Great Northern has vanished save for the crumbling remains of a red-brick bridge near the town's Leisure Centre though a fairly well-preserved bridge remains at Bestwood for those seeking out signs of this once busy coal-derived railway line which, surprisingly perhaps, survived as a going concern until as late as 1968.

In the same way that the Great Northern provided stations along its Derbyshire extension line and branches therefrom, passenger facilities were also incorporated into the Leen Valley system, these being at Bulwell Forest, Bestwood, Butlers Hill, Hucknall Town, Linby and Newstead. Linby thus gained a second passenger station, as already mentioned, that was quite literally only a hundred yards away from the rival Midland facilities. Even at the height of the railway age such duplication of facilities was hardly necessary especially for a tiny rural place like Linby.

One can't help but come to the conclusion that the G.N. included such stations purely as a public relations gesture. The directors could hardly have expected any of the stations along the line to provide enough passengers to justify their existence though there is no doubt that they probably came into their own with the occasional 'special' or holiday excursion. To return to Linby for a moment the reader will not be surprised to learn that this station was the first 'casualty' when its closure was announced in 1916. The reason given was that of a wartime economy measure. While this may be quite plausible one suspects that the First World War was used here as a convenient smokescreen to dispense with a 'white elephant'.

Hucknall Town station had been without regular passenger trains for a quarter of a century when this photograph was taken in the mid-1950s. Already the brickwork of Station Road bridge is showing signs of its age and the appearance of the booking office flanked between the two staircases is neglect personified. The station, its platforms and even the trackbed at this spot have vanished without trace, although interestingly, the Station Hotel survives and makes it possible to align oneself with the approximate spot today. The view is looking north towards Linby and immediately beyond the bridge the line is flanked by Thoresby Dale on the left and Linby Lane on the right.
Photo: Nottinghamshire County Council Leisure Services

The Great Northern, of course, was absorbed into the London and North Eastern Railway (L.N.E.R.) at the grouping of 1923 and eight years later regular passenger services were withdrawn completely from this route. The Dido, mentioned earlier, was purely a workmen's train and continued to pass this way for another 35 years.

Railway writer P. Howard Anderson in his 1973 book *Forgotten Railways of the East Midlands* recalls in a particularly evocative and entertaining way how the Great Northern network spread in the second half of the nineteenth century. In his account of the Leen Valley branch he paints a fascinating picture of the day-to-day operations over the railway; a line which throughout its life produced an endless procession of coal trains although in the years after the opening of the new Great Central, of which more in a moment, it provided a useful diversionary route to and from Nottingham and beyond.

Thus far the build up of the Leen Valley railway scenario in the closing decades of the 19th century is relatively straightforward. We have seen how the Midland Railway laid their rails through the valley towns en route to Mansfield and how, in due course, they were able to capitalize on the enormous growth in coal traffic generated by the

An afternoon mineral train from the Leen Valley pits to Colwick Yard is seen on the last leg of its journey through Arno Vale in the summer of 1955. The wagons are still passing beneath Arnot Hill Road bridge while the fireman leaning out is no doubt taking a few gulps of fresh air before the whole train disappears inside the stuffiness of Mapperley Plains tunnel. The ex-Great Central Robinson-designed engines, like the one pictured, were common performers on the Great Northern's Leen Valley extension and Colwick depot, in the fifties, was home to countless numbers of them! The location is now a footpath. Photo: C.A. Hill

opening out of the 'new' coalmines being sunk at the side of the railway.

We have also seen that the Midland enjoyed a monopoly on this highly lucrative traffic for some three decades. Then came the Great Northern who had already been active in the neighbouring Erewash Valley with its somewhat older coalfield. The Midland might have trailblazed the new line to Mansfield but the G.N. directors saw no reason why their company shouldn't share in the bonanza too. So they quickly planned, and built, their own railway which resulted in the Leen Valley coalowners having not one but two sources of transport for the huge coal reserves they were busy tapping.

From now on events move even more quickly . . . and the 1890s saw more and even bigger upheavals as yet another railway was set to appear on the Leen Valley map.

While the Midland Railway route continued to operate outside the politics of what was to emerge, that certainly can't be said of the Great Northern who were, by this time, becoming increasingly apprehensive about the manoeuvrings of the Manchester, Sheffield and Lincolnshire Railway based in Sheffield.

But first let it be said that the political posturings involved became complex, to say the least.

Since the purpose of this section of the book is to explain, as simply as possible to the reader, how the Leen Valley railway system developed it was felt appropriate to avoid delving too deeply into political complexities and thus confusing the issue. Many excellent books have already appeared dealing with the arrival of what emerged as the Great Central Railway and the student wishing to study the subject in greater depth is urged to refer to these.

In 1894, the first sod of the extension from Annesley to London was cut by the Countess of Wharncliffe, and it was hoped at the time that it would be ready for traffic in three years. This proved to be rather optimistic, for it was not until March 1899 that a regular passenger service was started. Arkwright Street and Carrington Street stations were used in Nottingham; the new Central station, or Victoria as it later became, was not finished until some time afterwards. Mr Edward Parry of Nottingham was the engineer in charge of the Rugby -Annesley section.

The coming of the Great Central into the Leen Valley at the very end of the 19th century meant the biggest upheaval yet seen as the main contractors Messrs Logan & Hemmingway set about the task of making a brand new trunk route on an almost 'no expense spared' basis. For whereas the original Midland route had passed through the valley relatively unobtrusively some forty-five years earlier with nothing more exciting in the way of civil engineering features than a series of timid level crossings the GC boldly set course southwards atop a long embankment stretching from Annesley almost down to Wighay Bridge at Bacon Springs on the northern boundary of Hucknall.

Trains setting off from Annesley first crossed Newstead Abbey drive on an ornate bridge similar to that provided by the Great Northern. For just short of a mile the GC ran adjacent to the GN and Midland lines . . . all three routes running parallel and within shouting distance of each other!

As Linby was approached, however, the new main line veered westwards and soon crossed the GN tracks on a tremendous lattice girder bridge just north of the GN's former Linby Station. Moments later trains ran over the Midland tracks on a somewhat less impressive deck. Again, after a couple of hundred yards, another bridge, squat and sturdy, carried the line across Wighay Road.

Heading south towards Hucknall the Great Central's new line ran on a falling gradient under Annesley Road and Washdyke Lane in quick succession before crossing over another substantial bridge that for years spanned only a footpath, a proper road not being built until housing development took place AFTER the line's final closure!

Suddenly, after riding high above the countryside, the line plunged into a deep cutting between Wood Lane and Watnall Road where, in the course of excavation, workmen dug into the course of a pre-historic river bed. Emerging from this cutting, trains ran into the first station on the new London extension route, Hucknall Central. The name related more to the title of the company than it did to any geographical implication for the station was actually the *least* central in terms of passenger convenience situated as it was nearly a mile out of town.

Hucknall Central was typical of stations on the London extension line with its 'island platform' and Jacobean style of architecture. The booking hall was at street level giving access to the platforms via a wooden deck above the up main line. Trains departing for Nottingham and beyond went on a falling gradient along the Leen Valley's western flank before arriving at Bulwell Hall Halt and soon afterwards passing over the magnificent 26-arch span of Bulwell viaduct the southern end of which heralded the approach to Bulwell Common station.

Bulwell Common, once again followed the usual 'island platform' and Jacobean style of achitecture and had a lot in common with

Hucknall Central . . . however it was a much busier place since as well as the passing to and fro of Great Central traffic there was also a junction at both ends of the station for the benefit of the Great Northern Railway. Quite a few additional 'transfer' sidings were

In the absence of any headboard at the front of the engine we have to assume this is not one of the Great Central's named trains but rather one of the regular cross country workings . . . possibly the Bournemouth - York service. This is a classic scene at Bulwell Common probably in the late 1950s when such sights were commonplace to residents in and about St. Alban's Road. The picture is worth dwelling on for a few moments longer not least to reflect upon the sheer weight of the train (do we count 12 bogies here?) when compared to modern train formations where just a couple of coaches is considered the norm for all but inter-city expresses. The B1 loco in charge, and its fireman in particular, clearly have their work cut out hauling this several hundred tons of coaches and passengers all the way ahead upgrade through Hucknall and Annesley. Judging by the exhaust the fireman has just got busy with his shovel after 'clearing' the bridge at the north end of Bulwell Common Station while the driver is no doubt keeping an anxious eye open for any more children like those on the embankment adjacent to the fifth coach. Just beyond the join of coaches four and five note the abutments of the small bridge spanning the footpath giving access to Bulwell Common itself (far left). The Gresley coach immediately behind the tender is noteworthy. Finally the picture also serves to illustrate in part the layout of the track formation at the north end of Bulwell Common station. Almost parallel with the far buffer of the B1 can be seen the Great Northern's 'up' line while on the extreme right centre the corresponding 'down' rails split from the Great Central, sweep round behind the photographer, pass underneath the Great Central metals and then rejoin the 'up-rails' . . . both continuing along the side of Bestwood Road on an embankment, crossing Hucknall Road by means of a Great Central-style bridge, before joining the original Great Northern Leen Valley line shortly afterwards. Photo: D. Swale

*Few planners could have guessed the extent to which road transport would develop when
this bridge reconstruction took place on Valley Road in the late 1930s. Both of these pictures
show the same site before and after the construction of a new bridge carrying the former
Great Central Railway over what is now the Nottingham ring road at Basford.*
Photo: Nottinghamshire County Council Leisure Services

provided here as a result.

At the northern end there was a flying underpass junction giving access to the Great Northern company's Leen Valley extension of 1882 while at the south end a flat junction linked the Great Central line with the Great Northern's Derbyshire extension route at Basford North station.

After Bulwell Common the GCR continued on a falling gradient through the Basford area with another station being provided at New Basford in Haydn Road . . . but this time instead of being below road level as at Hucknall and Bulwell the facilities at New Basford were above and passengers had to climb stairs to reach platform level.

As the line left New Basford the character of the route changed dramatically. The wide open spaces and fields around Annesley were exchanged for the outer suburbs of turn-of-the-century Nottingham. If you were aboard a train at the time, however, you would see little of the surroundings for immediately after New Basford the line plunged into Sherwood Rise tunnel, emerged briefly for air at Carrington station in a deep sandstone cutting, before burrowing again through Mansfield Road tunnel finally emerging at what has often been described as one of the most impressive stations in the

60939 New Basford, 9 August, 1963. This class of engine was a familar and stirring sight in the Leen Valley until the type disappeared in the mid sixties. Sherwood Rise tunnel's northern portal can be seen in the distance piercing the high ground. The entrance cutting is now full of houses and, allegedly, has a railway phantom!
Photo: M.S. Castledine

kingdom . . . Nottingham Victoria.

This route was indeed a great feat of railway engineering befitting its name and as far as the Leen Valley was concerned its civil engineering works brought a new dimension to the railway age. Not only that, but places like Basford, Bulwell and Hucknall that had previously been largely unheard of in the big outside world suddenly found themselves mentioned in main line railway timetables. Admittedly the important expresses did not actually stop at, say, Bulwell Common in the normal course of events . . . but at least they passed through. Hucknall was immortalized by Sir John Betjeman when the town received a mention in a poem he wrote about a journey on the Great Central.

And while it was under construction the line did receive a fair amount of attention from photographers . . . many pictures taken of the line being built in the 1890s have survived in collections that have subsequently been used to produce some of the numerous excellent books that have appeared, and continue to appear, about the Great Central.

One of these, L.T.C. Rolt's *The Making of a Railway* published in 1971 drew extensively on the record left for posterity by a young Leicester photographer S.W.A. Newton who visited sites along the route during the construction years between 1894-99. By the 1890s the average Victorian had become somewhat blasé about new railway construction. After all, he could hardly be expected to go on lauding the feats of the railway builders indefinitely. For a modern parallel, one has only to contrast the amount of interest and publicity which the construction and opening of our first motorway, the M1, attracted with the small attention that similar projects receive today.

The start of construction work in November 1894 brought scenes of destruction and apparent chaos to town and country alike which are comparable to modern motorway works. Swathes were cut through woodlands; crudely laid construction lines invaded the countryside and the inhabitants of hitherto remote cottages and farmsteads found their privacy rudely interrupted. From their windows they looked out on a wilderness of raw earth teeming with men and machines.

Earlier in our story of railway development in the Leen Valley we encountered the *Nottingham Review's* description of an early VIP trip along the mineral line operated by Messrs Wakefield and North of Cinderhill Colliery fame and noted that this occurrence may well have constituted the first-ever passenger train in the Leen Valley . . . even if the passengers were guests rather than fare-paying customers!

This was in 1844 at the very dawn of the steam railway age in Nottinghamshire.

Fifty-four years later another Nottingham publication called *City Sketches* wrote up details of a similar excursion for VIP's only this time to view work on the near-complete Great Central. In scale and magnitude the two projects were poles apart. But they were both railways and were both novelties of their period. The fledgling Nottingham Mineral Railway was a local affair intended to move coal to market or at least to a nearby waterway in the process, whereas the Great Central appeared a half century or so later in a world which had been turned upside down by the developments of the railway age.

The issue of *City Sketches* for 1 July, 1898, therefore, gives another fascinating glimpse into the past and records what may well have been the FIRST ever 'passenger' working out of Nottingham and up the Leen Valley to Annesley by way of the brand new and as yet unopened Great Central line.

In the following account one can almost smell the mortar drying on the brickwork inside Mansfield Road tunnel as the party is pulled through and, further along, imagine the gasps of admiration at the

92075 on the Bulwell Viaduct southbound, 12 May, 1965. Train and viaduct are now memories and the site is now presently occupied by Morrisons supermarket car park. The River Leen flowed beneath one of the arches to the rear of the scene.
Photo: M.S. Castledine

view afforded from the lofty heights of Bulwell Viaduct while others in the party would be studying the construction of the tall embankments further north, still raw earth and infill. Maybe here and there along the line they waved at workmen putting finishing touches to signal boxes or slapping protective paint onto bridge ironwork.

One thing we can be sure of is that the northbound 'excursion' would have travelled through a much less densely populated landscape then than a century later for the Nottingham of 1898 would have been left behind as the train passed New Basford. But on with the account which is headed simply 'The Great Central Railway'.

'There are few people residing in Nottingham, or indeed within a considerable distance of the ancient borough, who have not been very familiar with the fact that a great railway company has for some time past been engaged in the operation of constructing a new line of railway in their midst. Paragraphs in the newspapers purporting to describe the progress of the works, reports of arbitration cases of local interest and otherwise, and above all the demolition and disappearance of many well known land-marks, and the gradual evolving of order out of chaos have familiarized most of us with the visible and outward process of railway making; but how few comparatively speaking have the faintest notion or have ever taken the trouble to think of the many obstacles that have to be overcome, the difficult and delicate work that has to be performed and the possibilities which have to be provided against, to say nothing of the forethought and consideration entailed in the conception and formation of a line of railway through the heart of a great city.

'It was with the object of becoming more closely acquainted with the methods adopted in the construction of a modern railway that the excursion which took place on Saturday, 18th inst., was organized by the members of the staff of the City Engineer, who, by the courtesy of Mr Parry, the Chief Engineer, were afforded an opportunity of viewing the works included in the first contract of the Northern Division of the new line to London.

'The party assembled, as previously arranged, on the site of the new Central Station at about 2.45 in the afternoon, and occupied the time until the arrival of the engines and trucks, which had been kindly placed at their disposal by the contractors, Messrs. Logan & Hemingway, in inspecting the works there, where the platform walls and subways, and the foundations of the various buildings which are to be erected have already been put in; giving some slight indication how a large and important railway station, well fitted and lighted, may ultimately be developed out of what a few short months ago was nothing but a shapeless chasm, from which over half-a-million cubic yards of earthwork had been removed.

'The engine and trucks left the Central Station punctually at 3 o'clock, and conveyed the party without much preliminary warning into the tunnel which had been constructed under the Mansfield Road, and afterwards, with a short interval at Carrington Station, through the Sherwood Rise tunnel before emerging again into daylight at Haydn Road. Seated in an open truck travelling at a rapid rate through a dark and cold tunnel, with all the inconvenience of smoke and dust from the engine, is probably an experience to most of us more novel than agreeable, but upon emerging again into the open air one felt to some extent compensated by the exhilarating run to Annesley, and the opportunity thus afforded of viewing the surrounding country from the elevation of the train.

An unusual study to say the least! This photograph originally appeared in the Mansfield Chronicle Advertiser in October 1970 when the author was working as a journalist there. One of his assignments was to write a caption. Nearly 30 years on and history repeats itself! The picture is taken from the Annesley portal of the main Great Central tunnel beneath Robin Hood Hills and shows what looks like a Ford truck rumbling into the gloom with a load of infill, while beyond it looks like a sunny autumn day. The tunnel was infilled, so it was announced at the time, to enable half a million tons of coal to be worked out. This may well have been the case but whether it was necessary to continue this infill process in adjacent cuttings remains unclear. Regardless of the reasons the picture does illustrate what a thorough job someone felt it necessary to make of removing any remote possibility of the Great Central ever re-opening at some future time.
Photo: Mansfield Chronicle Advertiser

Annesley became famous for its allocation of British Railways Standard Class 9F freight locomotives and a Sunday visitor to Annesley shed in the late 1950s and early 1960s would see rows of them. Consequently photos taken at Annesley at this period always feature Standard Class 9F's rather prominently.
Photo: D. Dykes

Annesley locomotive depot might arguably have been called Newstead - mainly because that's where it was situated on the far side of Newstead Colliery yard and within a mile of Newstead Abbey, famous for its connections with the poet Lord Byron. Since the closure of the Great Central line as a through route in 1966 a goodly number of books have appeared - mainly photographic in content - chronicling this sadly short-lived main line to London. Oddly, though, few of them have captured the atmosphere of the line north of Nottingham and one or two in particular have wallowed in pictures of the route south of Leicester more or less ignoring the northern leg of the London extension. The loco sheds at Woodford Halse often appear in books on the Great Central but try finding any with illustrations of Annesley! Maybe, quite simply, photographers just didn't find it sufficiently interesting. This study of the shed apron probably dates from about 1959 and is notable for capturing a former North Eastern Railway B16 4-6-0 on the right. The three tenders facing the camera belong to a trio of the large allocation of 9F 2-10-0 freight engines famous for their performances with the Annesley to Woodford 'runners' or 'windcutters' that continued to operate over the line until 1965. Note also the front end of the rebuilt class '01' while an unidentified loco lurks in the background.
Photo: N.E. Stead

45333 and 44665 in Annesley Shed 11 September, 1965.
Photo: M.S.Castledine

Fireman Geoff Clarke (left) with shunters Albert Cleverly and Fred Smith at Annesley in the summer of 1957. Geoff, who lived in Bulwell at the time, clearly recalls the day he saw the 'Flying Bedstead' on trial at Hucknall Aerodrome while riding on the footplate of a southbound coal train. 'I pointed it out to my driver,' said Geoff. 'From up on the railway embankment we had a good view over the airfield and there was this strange Meccano-like contraption hovering just off the ground.' Geoff Clarke ended his railway days at Toton depot after the closure of Annesley.

Ray Clarke was a fireman at Annesley but upon closure of the depot he moved to Rolls Royce at Hucknall. In this 1958 view, Ray sits in the foreground upon his shovel, flanked by shunter/setter Lou Britton (left) and driver Sam Hubbard (right).

Although undated, it is a pretty fair bet that this study of Britannia class 4-6-2 No.70014 'Iron Duke' dates from about 1962. Annesley received the cast-offs from other routes where dieselization or electrification was ousting steam traction and a visitor to the sheds in the early to mid 1960's might expect to see not only Britannia class locomotives but former L.M.S. express types as well. 'Iron Duke' appears to be obscuring a Thompson Class B1 4-6-0 standing on the shed apron. The entire site at Annesley after closure was buried forever under a mountain of colliery waste and not a trace remains of depot or sidings.
Photo: D. Dykes

The 'Midlandization' of the Great Central section in 1958 may have been greeted with mixed feelings by railway workers . . . but it brought about some remarkable changes to delight 1960s schoolboy 'spotters. The mundane freight-only nature of Annesley depot was transformed within a couple of years by some unlikely arrivals including former L.M.S. Royal Scot and Jubilee class locomotives as well as a sprinkling of rebuilt Patriot types. Even a few Britannia class representatives made Annesley their home, albeit briefly. However, far from trying to glamorize Annesley's role, the powers that be were merely dumping these engines on the Great Central as they became redundant through dieselization or electrification elsewhere. One visitor to Annesley shed was Stanier Jubilee Class 5XP No. 45567 'South Australia' seen here one Sunday morning with the author Martin Weiss, in school blazer, enjoying a crafty view from the driver's side while his younger brother, Robert, is pondering the distance back to ground level. At this period it was commonplace to see formerly named locomotives running on the Great Central with their nameplates removed leaving just a backing plate.
Photo: Roy Weiss

The Great Central moved coal south from the pits in North Derbyshire and South Yorkshire as far as Annesley marshalling yards where trains were re-sorted for their onward journeys. The comings and goings of this traffic went on largely unnoticed by the general public simply because it became such a familiar sight on the landscape. This study of an ex-WD 2-8-0 freight loco clanking its way towards Annesley past Kirkby Bentinck seems, retrospectively, a reminder of those fondly remembered days of the 1950s and early 1960s when nobody even remotely suspected the changes that lay ahead for the railways. To the rear of the train is the footbridge linking Church Hill with Mill Lane while further to the rear is the bridge carrying the lower part of Church Hill over the Great Central tracks immediately south of Kirkby Bentinck platforms. In the left foreground is the rail access into Bentinck Colliery. In this instance we have strayed very slightly out of the Leen Valley, for this particular part of the Great Central ran briefly along the northern flank of the Erewash Valley where, apart from serving Bentinck Colliery, the GCR also had a short branch line into nearby Langton Colliery.
Photo: D. Dykes

'Upon arriving at Annesley, where the London Extension of the Great Central Railway commences by a junction with the existing Derbyshire line of the Company, the party detrained and walked back along the line for the distance of about a mile, inspecting en route the new gravitation sidings which have been laid down for the purpose of marshalling and sorting the trains coming from the Derbyshire and South Yorkshire coalfields, an area of about sixty acres having been purchased by the company for that purpose. A large engine shed and wagon repairing shop, with all the necessary offices and workshops have been erected here; and from this point the coal and goods trains will run through to similar sidings at Woodford in Northamptonshire, and so on to Neasden, a suburban station in the north of London, where arrangements will be made for receiving and distributing this traffic.

'Upon again joining the engine near the bridge over the Newstead Abbey Drive, which owing to is proximity to the historic Abbey has been made of a very ornamental character, the party was conveyed at a somewhat slower rate to the Hucknall Town Station, where a short halt was made to allow of the inspection of the station buildings. Proceeding towards Nottingham the line is carried over the Midland Railway and River Leen by a high viaduct, immediately south of which the Bulwell Common Station has been erected, and the branch lines which are being constructed jointly with the Great Northern Company with a view to giving access to the Leen Valley and Derbyshire lines of that company join the Great Central Railway at this point. A little further south is another junction which has been made for the purpose of enabling the Great Northern Company to run its trains from Burton, Stafford, and Derby, over the Great Central Railway into the Nottingham Central Station which is owned jointly by both Companies.

'The next stopping place was the station named after the busy and growing district it is intended mainly to serve, New Basford, where a large shed for the purpose of cleaning and storing carriages is being erected, and where a building with the necessary retorts, machinery and appliances for the manufacture of oil-gas for the lighting of the carriages is being provided. Having again passed through Sherwood Rise Tunnel, Carrington Station was reached. This will be the ticket station for the north, and will be a great convenience to the large population residing at this end of the city. Nottingham Central Station next engaged the attention of the party, and a short stop was made here to afford an opportunity of a further examination of the progress of the work. This station, as previously remarked, will be the

Standard Class 9F 2-10-0 No.92200 was not one of the original members of the 'windcutter' fleet to be based at Annesley depot and it may well be that this view of Kirkby South Junction dates from 1964 or 1965 - very close to the end as far as all three lines in this view are concerned. The train itself - a very long rake of hoppers - is snaking off the so-called Mansfield Railway route onto the Great Central main line and the engine is just about to pass under the bridge carrying the unadopted road from Kirkby-in-Ashfield to Nuncargate. The loco tender, brake van and first wagon are straddling the pointwork leading off to the Great Northern Leen Valley extension route to Sutton-in-Ashfield and Shirebrook. Viewed from a modern perspective perhaps one of the most interesting features of this scene is that having been totally infilled since closure the new Robin Hood line from Nottingham to Mansfield now follows almost exactly the Great Northern curve to the right . . . although the modern line is up on an embankment rather than down in a cutting!
Photo: D. Dykes

Just 'over the hill' as it were from Annesley yards and on the other side of the tunnel was Kirkby South Junction . . . a busy spot where both the Great Northern's Leen Valley route continued on towards Sutton-in-Ashfield, Skegby and Shirebrook (see left of signal box) and the so-called Mansfield Railway also joined the GC main line. This picture dates from the summer of 1962 and shows a class 9F 2-10-0 about to move off from a stop at the signal box no doubt on its way to Annesley sheds. Clearly seen on the skyline are the houses atop Shoulder of Mutton Hill, the highest point in Nottinghamshire and also reputed to be the loftiest place between Annesley church spire due east and the Ural mountains in Russia!.
Photo: Peter Wharmby

joint property of the Great Central and the Great Northern Railway Companies. It occupies an area of about twelve acres of land which was formerly covered for the greater part by a dense population living mostly in small tenements and under extremely unsanitary conditions; and if for no other reason, the fact that this unwholesome area has been demolished from the centre of the city, and will be replaced by a new and imposing edifice should, one would think, entitle the Railway Company to the consideration and gratitude of even those of the inhabitants of Nottingham, who look upon the line as an unsightly and unwelcome innovation.'

The sharp-eyed reader will have spotted a reference towards the end of the account of the train pausing at Hucknall Town station where the group inspected the station buildings . . . this, of course, is Hucknall Central which had, at the time, not quite become 'Central' and likewise the departure from the Central station at Nottingham would have meant Nottingham Victoria as it became soon afterwards.

And so it came to pass that by the turn of the 20th century the Leen Valley railway map assumed the form that it would take for the next six or seven decades although it can be fairly said that the high-water mark of railways in this part ot Nottinghamshire was certainly during and immediately after the Edwardian period leading up to the Great War of 1914-18.

The only significant 'casualty' was the closure of the Basford to Bennerley line as a through route. This occurred during the war and some of the track thus salvaged was earmarked for service in France. But this move was thwarted, evidently, when the ship taking it across the channel was sunk!

Modern residents of Hucknall will no doubt be amazed to discover that in 1927, for example, the town boasted what a local guidebook described as 'railway facilities unsurpassed by any town of its size in the country.' By this time a new generation would be emerging who would never have known the town without its labyrinth of railway lines and to them the constant procession of trains and the non-stop activity of rail traffic around the pits would have been an everyday backdrop to the Leen Valley at work.

Even so the guidebook, which was produced mainly to encourage businesses to move to the town, announced proudly that no fewer than ONE HUNDRED passenger trains called at Hucknall every day of the week at one or other of the local stations and don't forget this wasn't the grand total of passenger trains that could be seen since some passed through without stopping and they didn't count!

This state of affairs continued up until 1931 when the ending of stopping trains on the former Great Northern route proved to be the first crack in the railways' fabric.

In his book *Hills of Annesley* Canon Frank Lyons describes well what it was like at the very top of the Leen Valley as a result of the railway age.

'These (railway) developments,' he writes 'changed the character of the upper Leen Valley beyond recognition. Throughout history it had been an agricultural backwater, neglected because there was no convenient outlet to the north. A man on horseback could mount the hills but the carts which carried the produce of the farms could not. The few scattered farms on the Newstead or Annesley estates could be reached, for farming purposes, only from the valley to the south. All of it had been a part of Sherwood Forest and its main use had been for hunting the foxes living on the hillside, the deer being among the trees. But in the 19th century and in the course of one generation, all was transformed. Collieries were sunk, houses were built and the district wrapped in a maze of railway lines.'

As well as undertaking a major rebuilding scheme at Nottingham station the Midland Railway also invested in a lavish new station at Hucknall. The old 1848 station and level crossing was swept away and a brand new facility created just a few yards south of the original site. A substantial new bridge was also erected. With its island style platform, blue-brick bridge and comfortable passenger facilities, the Midland had, effectively, copied the Great Central who had not long opened their station at Watnall Road. The photograph shows a Nottingham-bound train arriving from the Mansfield direction and the study probably dates from 1904 when the new station opened. Sadly these magnificent buildings were demolished in the 1960s but the Robin Hood service still operates here . . . though passengers in winter are no longer afforded a cosy waiting room with a roaring fire. Not all progress is for the better!
Photo: Nottinghamshire County Council Leisure Services

The railways, he suggested, transformed the lives of women and girls. Low fares were charged because profits were made from freight, principally coal. The passenger services, though they paid their way and ran at a small profit, were an extra. The growing knitwear industry could absorb the girls when they left school and employ them until they married, when it was traditional for them to take care of their homes, their husbands, and their children. In such ways, went on Canon Lyons, the railways loosened the social fabric. Girls, accustomed to travelling about the district, had a wider choice for husbands. If they married out of their own village, the trains brought them back with their babies, to visit their parents and did so cheaply. Women took their shopping bags and went off to the markets in Nottingham or Mansfield where there was a far greater choice than in the local shops. And in a time when few working people could afford an annual holiday away from home, the railways ran cheap excursions on Sundays, giving miners and factory workers four hours by the sea. In summer, the trains were packed.

It was in that inter-war period (1919-1938) that public transport reached its peak of efficiency and convenience. The roads were not clogged with traffic; the local trains were frequent and cheap, and in the towns trams ran along all the major roads carrying people to every district.

'One of the causes for this past age seeming so attractive was the existence of competition. In the Leen Valley, with the railways running almost side by side and each village having more than one station, the whole staff from the stationmaster to the newest porter were aware of the competition and made their stations as attractive as they could with beds of flowers and hanging baskets in summer and blazing fires in the waiting-rooms in winter. Incredible as it may now seem, they knew their regular passengers and made them welcome. The companies, too, tried to look their best. In particular they took a pride in their engines, the only dirty ones being on goods trains. The Midland trains gleamed in deep crimson from engine to guard's van, contrasting with the sturdy black and green of the Northern. The Central, being the last to arrive, had to try the hardest. It brought long-distance trains through the district, their routes displayed on boards along the roofs of the carriages. Expresses from Manchester to London were the commonest, but more exotic trains passed through each day, such as boat trains from Lancashire to Ipswich, or holiday trains from Aberdeen to Penzance. Such expresses brought a touch of class to the district as they rushed by the local trains at greater speed.

'It was a world which seemed unshakable, a part of the fabric of life which nothing would change, but it all vanished within a few years. In 1960 the Central sidings at Annesley, eighteen for the down line and nineteen for the opposite direction, were still handling a heavy traffic of coal, iron and steel, fish and fruit. There were eighty arrivals from the north each day and sixty-four departures; and to the south forty-seven arrivals and sixty-four departures. Many men were employed, drivers, firemen, guards and signalmen, to keep this traffic moving and fitted into the flow of passenger traffic, both distant and local, which ran along the line. But in a matter of a few years it was all gone. Freight traffic came to an end in June, 1965 and the Central line closed entirely in September, 1966.

'The other lines fared little better. The Northern passenger trains had ceased in 1931 and the coal trains ended in 1968. The tunnels under the Robin Hood Hills were closed to save maintenance. All the passenger stations closed within a few years of each other. When the mines are exhausted the railways will have gone, too, and even now most of the coal moves by road,' writes Canon Lyons.

Earlier we noted how, by the turn of the 20th century, the Leen Valley railway map had stabilized after the last big upheaval created by the Great Central's arrival in the late 1890s . . . this is true in the context of the old-style private railway companies but we cannot afford to ignore one final fling at railway building that, surprisingly, didn't materialize until as late as the early 1950s. For the relatively newly-formed British Railways wanted to carve their initials into the Leen Valley sandstone, too!

Was there any room left for another line of railway?

In the normal north-south corridor almost certainly not. Scarcely a spare inch of land remained that wasn't sprawling with sidings or cluttered with mine buildings or sulphurous spoil tips. Quite clearly any new route would have to go clear of the Leen Valley to find any space . . . and in 1952 this is precisely what happened when the last 'navvies' completed yet another great railway.

Yet the very building of this latecomer on the railway map created something of a puzzle for railway observers. For, although it was laid down ostensibly to service the newly-opened mine at Calverton, there were certain features about its construction that seemed odd.

For a start the entire line from Bestwood to Calverton was built to main line standards with *double track* throughout its length. Next, both the former Midland route *and* the Great Northern were allowed access to the new line, this in itself is odd since one must remember that in a 'nationalized' scenario there would have been no purpose in 'competing' lines needing access when one would have been enough. Also, to control this important new junction at Bestwood/Butler's Hill a new signal box was installed to control the amount of points and signals that became necessary to handle the anticipated flow of traffic not to mention 'up' and 'down' transfer sidings. Bridges and other civil engineering features were all built very sturdily. But, remember, we're only talking about trains to ONE coal mine. Granted Calverton's projected output of one million tons a year was a substantial contribution to the area's output but one pit would hardly justify such lavish rail facilities and certainly not a double track main line. Or was the newly-formed National Coal Board dreaming that Calverton would eventually be producing coal so prolifically that a constant half-hourly frequency of trains would be necessary to move away the coal?

If we study other modern pits in the Nottinghamshire coalfield that came on stream in the post-war years (Bevercotes and Cotgrave spring to mind) we find no comparable rail facilities. They just had single track branch lines to serve them as did all the other pits in the area that weren't immediately adjacent to a convenient existing line.

Returning for a moment to Messrs Coxon & Birks and their late 1940's work *Railway Development in the Nottinghamshire Coalfield* we discover the following enlightening passage:

'In addition to the newly opened Bilsthorpe colliery, new pits were contemplated at Calverton, south of Blidworth, and Bothamsall, north of Ollerton; and it is evident to the railway companies that lines must be built to serve them.

'The outcome was a proposed railway line some twenty-four miles long to be constructed and controlled jointly by the L.M.S. and L.N.E.R. Authorized in 1926, it was to extend from junctions with the L.M.S. and L.N.E.R. at Hucknall, through Farnsfield and Ollerton to Checker House on the L.N.E.R. between Worksop and Retford. Work was not started in earnest until the Autumn of 1929, when the building of the seven mile middle section between Ollerton and Farnsfield was undertaken by Shanks and McEwan, the Scottish firm of contractors. This was completed and opened about 1930, and the only loop is at Bilsthorpe. The signal box here was manned by L.M.S. staff, and before it was opened in 1931, the points were operated from ground frames. Although the line was single, enough ground was acquired for *double track*, and the work involved the excavation of some 922,000 cubic yards of cutting, the construction of twenty-four bridges, and a viaduct.

'This section was the only part of the project to be completed, and

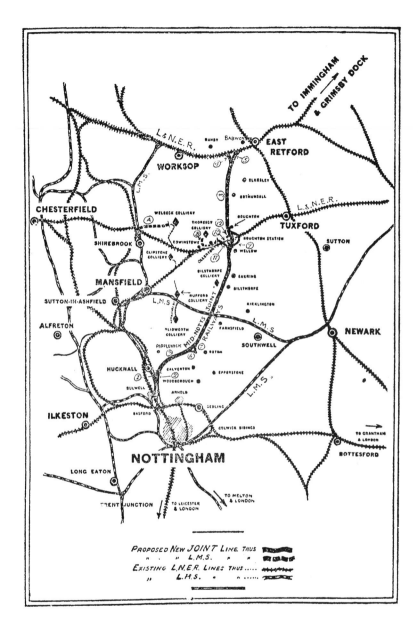

An old map of the Nottingham (north) railway system showing the route of the proposed Mid-Notts Joint Line, Part-built piecemeal, this line was never completed although the Calverton 'branch' built in the early 1950s would seem to have been a late but abortive attempt to do so.

Photo: Nottinghamshire County Council Leisure Services.

it is doubtful whether the northern and southern extensions will ever be built, for neither of the proposed pits were sunk'.

A reporter with the *Nottingham Journal* wrote in October 1927: 'Some fifteen months have now passed since Parliament sanctioned the scheme promoted jointly by the London & North Eastern Railway (who took over the former Great Northern Railway, author) and the London, Midland and Scottish Railway (who absorbed the former Midland Railway) for the construction of a new railway over about twenty-four miles of country from a point near Hucknall to Checker House near East Retford.'

Old newspaper cuttings can be fascinating sources of information . . . and we're eager to discover what else the Journal's reporter unearthed!

'The new railway is projected to run from near Bestwood Colliery (on a course about midway between Papplewick and Calverton) to Bilsthorpe and thence to Ollerton and the main line at Checker House.

'There will be a *DOUBLE LINE* (author's italics) and its main purpose is to cater for the several new collieries either coming into being or about to be commenced. At the same time it will serve as a *passenger* line between Retford and Nottingham.'

The *Journal* reporter's investigation revealed, also, that there was a certain measure of agitation among coal owners along the proposed route of the railway because nothing visible was happening. 'There is no spade work done in connection with the scheme,' one colliery owner is reported to have said. 'The matter is giving serious concern to my company. Nothing of account has been done yet.'

Among other gems of information in the same report was the revelation that the Babbington Company (presumably the Cinderhill concern) was seriously looking into a new sinking at Oxton village which would, of course, have been on the direct line of the proposed railway.

The September 1950 issue of the National Coal Board's 'Coal' magazine devoted a page-and-a-half to an account of work starting on the line to Calverton. The writer here was clearly more interested in the public relations appeal of the proposed engineering work but, nonetheless, the article makes entertaining reading and also nicely rounds off our chapter on the Leen Valley railways. It reads:

'COAL IS THE ONLY PASSENGER'

'A new railway is a rare event in Britain but one is being built across seven miles of Notts countryside, to carry, not passengers, but a million tons of coal a year from Calverton's new colliery through to the main lines at Bulwell.'

On a shining wet summer morning, stocky Cyril Waltham climbed into the seat of his big red bulldozer, started the machine, set it to tearing up a long strip of green turf. Just another job of work for him but the first step in bringing to realisation blueprints which have been on paper for nearly twenty-six years.

Thus began one of the biggest projects for a new railway in Britain for a long time. Seven miles of *double track* (author's italics) linking the new colliery at Calverton with the main Midland and North-Eastern lines at Bulwell, near Nottingham. When the pit has reached full production the new track will carry a million tons of coal a year. And the lines will cut clean across meadows and woodlands that were once a part of Sherwood Forest.

Plans began in 1926.

First talks on building the new railway began in 1926, when a private company interested in sinking a new shaft by the Old Rufford

The Calverton 'branch' had been reduced to single track by the 1970s though this study of the bridge near Papplewick Pumping Station clearly shows the vacant space where the second set of rails once were. Note also the sheer size of the bridge which, to add to the puzzle, carries only a little-used country lane even today. The Calverton line appears to abound in such extravagances. Mining subsidence has badly affected the track bed near Calverton in recent years.
Photo: Author

Road, some six miles from Nottingham, wanted to link up their proposed pit site with the main lines to the south. Those plans reached a fair stage of development, but finally fell through because of strikes and financial problems. Ten years later the plans for a new railway were revived; this time to serve the B.A. Collieries' projected new shaft at Calverton. Then came the Second World War, the nationalization of the mines, and the emergence of the present scheme.

All of this time the practical details from the mining point of view were watched by tall, shrewd L.H. Spencer, now Chief Surveyor to No. 6 Area, East Midlands Division (N.C.B). One of the officials concerned in the original project twenty-four years ago, it must have been a great day for him when the engineers finally went into action this summer.

Colonel C.D. Suffolk, British Railways Engineer in charge of the job, is a cheerful modest man. He describes the cutting of these seven miles of track as 'just a routine job' plenty of hard work, but no special problems'.

But the detailed plans tell an impressive story. The earthworks contract, for example, consists of moving nearly one-and-a-half million tons of earth and sandstone. Scrapers, powered by large crawler-tractors with diesel engines, will cut as deep as fifty feet into the high ground.

Where the material has to be taken over long distances, huge, diesel-powered, rubber-tyred units will be used to haul a special type of scraper outfit. Excavators will also be used, especially where hard sandstone rock is encountered. On certain stretches the material may have to be blasted loose.

There will be two diversions of the dark, sluggish River Leen where local fishermen claim good catches of trout and crayfish. A new bridge will be built to carry the railway over the river.

Local legend has it that the Bulwell stream, at the Nottingham end of the new line, has magic qualities: that water first began to flow after a bull had struck a large rock with his horns. Magic or not, the Bulwell stream will be prosaically piped under the railway lines.

At one point the new line will cut across a busy allotment, and then neatly through a pig-sty. At another, it will be necessary to drive half a mile through a fir forest planted by the Forestry Commission. A row of pegs, a foot high, marks out the route of the line across the countryside. Through this forest woodsmen have already cleared a path 15 feet wide. Before the excavators drive through, this path will be extended to a width of 80 feet, for the railway will run some thirty feet in a cutting below the forest.

Two bridges will be built to carry public roads over the track, including the diversion of the main Nottingham-Mansfield road. Two other bridges will carry the railway over public roads. These jobs have some tough and tricky problems attached. When the engineers come to divert the main road they will be cutting across the huge pipeline carrying the entire water supply to the population of Nottingham. But the housewives of that thriving city will find their taps running dry for only a matter of hours and not days, for the entire stretch of new roadway, complete with arched bridge and an alternative water pipeline, will be constructed before the old road is cut. The existing water pipeline will then be closed and diverted through the new system, giving only a brief shut-off.

Mrs C.D. Suffolk, wife of the Railways' Resident Engineer, using a silver-plated spade, cut the first sod at a formal ceremony in July. Now the scheme is going rapidly ahead. But though a great scar is appearing across the green Nottinghamshire hills and meadows as the plan takes shape, the top soil stripped in the work is being carefully preserved. When the job is completed, this soil will be spread over the surface of the embankments and cuttings, and resown with grass to heal the scars.

Formally, the official description of the new railway says that the tracks will be known as Calverton Colliery Branch (Railway No. 1 and Railway No. 2). Railway No. 1, approximately seven miles long, will start from a point on the Nottingham-Mansfield (L.M.R.) line and finish near the Calverton Lodge, on the road to Oxton. Railway No. 2, approximately half a mile long, will connect Railway No. 1 with the Leen Valley line (Eastern Region) near where the latter crosses the Nottingham-Mansfield line (L.M.R.).

About seventeen miles of permanent way will be laid in sidings and the branch railway. The work will be progressively completed from the point where it joins the main line, so that it will be possible for the great precast slabs of concrete and pre-fabricated steel girders for the bridges to be carried direct to the sites by rail.

The new shunting yards to link up with the railway will be built in a valley at the rear of Calverton pit. They will be of the most modern type, and serviced by diesel mechanical locomotives.

What of the men on the job? Cyril Waltham, who tore up that first green strip is typical. Bluff and hard working, with his home at Radcliffe-on-Trent, he has worked for twelve years on general construction and demolition jobs. He pointed out that not one man in a hundred who would be working on the laying of the railway had ever done a similar job before.

'Building a railway across new country is something that happens so seldom nowadays that very few of the men will have had the chance of trying it before,' he said. 'A few might have done it in the Army if they were abroad during the war, but that would be all. Personally, I only worked once before on constructing a railway. That was twelve years ago on a line to a new factory in Scotland.

'Although no passenger traffic will be carried, the coming of the new line to Calverton will complete the transformation of the rural village, already much changed by the rapid devolpments at the pit. A few years ago Calverton was a tiny old-fashioned hamlet famed for hand-made stockings, its ancient industry, whose many looms could be seen through the high, wide upper windows of the local cottages.

'The old order is vanishing now, but it will be replaced, the planners are confident, by a model industrial township as fine as the 20th century can produce.'

Anyone who cares to study the Calverton Colliery 'branch' today - and there is no better way than to footslog along part or all of its length - may well conclude that this apparently main line formation WAS intended to aspire to something more than a humble coal corridor for just one mine.

Could it be that the Leen Valley was denied its fourth major rail route arising from post-Second World War financial restraints?

Perhaps somewhere in a vault beneath Whitehall lies a dusty file confirming that no further contracts would be let for construction of the Mid-Notts line beyond Calverton Colliery.

COAL

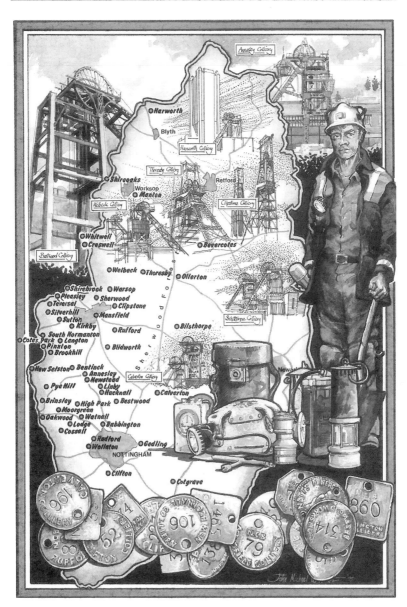

A print showing the former extent of the Nottinghamshire coalfield. The Leen Valley district is lower left in the above illustration.
Courtesy: John Michael Webster

BY 1900 THE SMALL towns and villages from Wilford and Radford near the River Trent to Annesley and Newstead some nine miles further north had been transformed from quiet farming and stocking-frame economies into busy coalmining centres.

Meadows and woodlands disappeared as pit headstocks reared up in their place along with coal preparation plant buildings, stocking sites and miles of railway sidings. And even then more and more space had to be found to dump the huge volumes of waste material being generated by an expanding coalfield.

In the years immediately preceding the Great War of 1914-1918 when coal production in the Leen Valley — and pretty well everywhere else — was at its zenith, huge spoil heaps were raised and continued to grow bigger and loftier so that a visitor looking upon them from a distance might imagine he was looking upon a cluster of conical pyramids.

As the decades passed and the 1950's period arrived the topography of the district resembled a somewhat prehistoric scenario. The spoil tips, which rose up all over the valley, often suffered from partial combustion and at night the effect created was dramatic giving places like Bestwood and Hucknall a surreal atmosphere as the glow from these high-up fires lit up the sky for miles around after the fashion of a volcanic eruption!

Linby Colliery shortly before closure - a nocturnal study of a now vanished site. The pit was a European productivity leader in 1963 in which year 1,113 men produced 1,325,675 tons. Photo: Peter Stevenson

On foggy February afternoons thousands of domestic chimneys belched forth thick plumes of greenish brown coal smoke adding to the sulphurous discharges from the burning tips while an endless procession of dingy trains clanked and crawled about their business sending further eruptions of smoke and steam into the long-suffering local atmosphere.

It was not a scene likely to impress the modern student of environmental health, yet to most residents of the Leen Valley communities after the end of the Second World War this was everyday state of play. King Coal, after a century of dominance, still reigned supreme and, despite its visual shortcomings and despoliation of the land, the industry provided work for thousands both directly and indirectly.

By day the district echoed to the crash and clatter of railway wagons being shunted in the nearest siding or pit yard; by night the population slept through the din for it went on just the same. The early hours of cold midwinter nights sometimes gave an added clarity to the sounds of the Leen Valley at work; the slow beat of a winding engine at work here, the ponderous thud and wheezing of a railway engine there, the rattle and clang of coal trucks and the muffled sounds of machinery from within buildings somewhere in the darkness.

The Leen Valley was dotted with coalmines by 1960 and all were linked by a confusing web of railway lines. The 1947 State takeover of the industry — popularly known as 'Nationalization' — brought with it within a few years a massive Government-funded investment programme. The upper Leen Valley mines in particular were to benefit from this largesse, the express intention of which was to expand output and improve productivity, for the 1939-45 war had left most coalmines in a rundown state.

Millions were lavished on underground productivity-improving schemes. For example there was rapid progress in moving coal production out of the pick and shovel era as coalfaces became mechanized. Huge drilling machines that had to be taken down below in bits and then re-assembled revolutionized the work of driving headings and opening out new seams. Ventilation systems were improved and underground haulage was modernized; pit ponies were pensioned off.

Eventually more millions were ploughed into surface modernization schemes and the visual appearance of some pits altered dramatically from their pre-war look. Notable surface rebuilding took place at Babbington, Hucknall, Linby and

Pitmen enjoy a police 'escort' in the street at Newstead while another study shows a massed meeting just outside the pit gates in the 1926 general strike. Views of Leen Valley pits from this period are rare and this one in particular shows the surface buildings prior to modernization. . . and (below) Newstead's final surface appearance circa. 1980.
Photo: J.Archer

Newstead. Hucknall Colliery in particular was totally rebuilt during a rolling programme of investment in the late 1950s and early 1960s. The new towering concrete headstocks that loomed over the Portland Road area of town could be seen for miles and a walker on the Misk Hills looking down would wonder at this vulgar concrete intrusion on the landscape.

Along with the new-look pit came a palatial miners' welfare institute. In terms of size and the facilities it offered this new centre alone was a marvel; a monument to the new prosperity and standards for Leen Valley pitmen. The new welfare centre wasn't just for Hucknall. It was also to be shared with Linby and thus it became the Hucknall/Linby Miners' Welfare Institute. The pit and its social facilities were a national showpiece and people from well outside the district came to Hucknall just to sightsee! The colliery became the first in Europe to enjoy coalface lighting.

In Nottinghamshire the drive for more coal and better productivity didn't end with modernizing old pits. Three new mines were brought into production and while the sinkings at Cotgrave and Bevercotes are outside the scope of this particular study the third, at Calverton, can fairly be admitted as a Leen Valley pit. Calverton, unlike the other two new sinkings, was planned and partly developed under private enterprise but the intervention of the Second World War meant that the bulk of the development work was carried out by the National Coal Board (NCB).

With such colossal investment the Leen Valley towns were, by the mid-1960s, confident that coal would continue to generate local prosperity for at least another century. The politicians were saying so and so, too, were Coal Board chiefs. A job in mining was a job for life. Sons would still follow their fathers into the pits. All seemed settled and assured.

The early sixties proved to be, in retrospect, a kind of Indian Summer for the coal industry and, for that matter, for the railway network that relied upon it for business. Nobody, of course, even guessed this at the time and there was no real indication of trouble on the horizon. Some of the Leen Valley's 'star' pits were hitting a million tons a year output with regular ease and there was much satisfaction in high places that the money invested earlier was now paying off.

Certainly nobody could forsee in 1965 the dramatic decline which would occur over the next two decades or so. At about this time a few of the older pits at the bottom of the district including Wollaton and Radford had gone out of production, but such closures did not really sound any alarm bells because such pits were understood to be life-expired anyway. Even the closure of Clifton Colliery in the late 1960s and on the very banks of the River Trent at its confluence with the Leen did not attract much attention outside the immediate locality. Of course there were always efforts made to reverse closure decision plans but it is important to remember that at this period men displaced by the closure of Clifton, Radford and Wollaton could be easily absorbed into the workforce at other nearby mines.

Among what might be termed the big mines there was only one 1960s' casualty and this came at Bestwood and again for those men who wished to remain within the industry there were still plenty of opportunities elsewhere in the district. Many pitmen took advantage of transfer terms.

At this point it might be a worthwhile exercise to pause and look at what was happening in the coal industry in the big wide world OUTSIDE the Leen Valley district. For many less prosperous coalfields like those in the North East, Shropshire, Staffordshire and even as close as Derbyshire the 1960's were definitely not good times. In Derbyshire, for example, the older Erewash Valley coalfield suffered severely from closures to the point where a once coalmine-infested area was left with just one single operational pit, Ormonde Colliery near Heanor. One-time substantial concerns like the Shipley

A 1960 study of Bestwood Colliery which might have been taken to impress judges in a Best Kept Colliery contest! Notice how the mine blends into the local countryside, a common feature of pits in the Leen and Erewash valleys. Pithead winding gear still survives as a kind of mining memorial at the entrance to Bestwood Country Park, but of the rest of the buildings no trace remains.

Collieries (Woodside and Coppice) near Ilkeston went out of production and even the smaller affairs like Cossall, again close to Ilkeston, were shut. It is probably no exaggeration to say that pits were being axed so frequently and so fast that the whole business was in danger of losing its news value.

Certainly at least some of the pits that went under Harold Wilson's Labour Government of the mid-1960s were loss-makers anyway or at any rate were running out of reserves or were encountering difficult geographical conditions to the point where they were unprofitable to keep open. This is a fact of life in coalmining. No pit can last forever. But that having been said, an awful lot of coalmines were lost in the 1960s and many observers have cast doubt on the above reasons being the REAL cause of mass closures. Some commentators pointed to coal's future as a national energy resource becoming increasingly thwarted by political pressures. The finger was being pointed at oil.

It is true to say that during the first Wilson government from 1964 coal markets were being eroded by the development of (uneconomic) nuclear power stations, the resurgence of the gas industries with the importation of natural gas and the discovery of North Sea resources along with the prospect of North Sea oil giving

Clifton Colliery, probably during the Edwardian years on Trentside.
Photo: Notts County Council Leisure Services

confidence to potential oil-fired boiler installations.

By the late 1960s Britain was awash with cheap Middle East oil to the point where it was cheaper to use the imported fuel than to mine it at home ... cheaper for the State at any rate who now controlled the coal industry. This line of thinking was dramatically demonstrated by the wholesale destruction of Britain's huge fleet of steam railway locomotives in favour of diesel traction. It is true that Britain's railways needed modernizing but there emerged a sudden urgency to accelerate the process to the point where steam locomotives that were nearly brand-new were being unceremoniously cut up with those built in the 19th century.

Parts of the old Great Northern Railway system in Bulwell were used as dumps for these redundant steamers. They were being pulled out of service faster than scrapyards could break them up in 1964 and consequently the depressing sight of rusting hulks in weed infested sidings became commonplace at Rigley's wagon works on Bulwell Common, in sidings at Leen Valley Junction at the back of the City Hospital and further along at Daybrook.

They provided a marvellous albeit temporary adventure playground for kids living in Arnold Road and thereabouts. Workmen

Re-built 'Patriot' class No. 45535 'Sir Herbert Walker KCB' was one of many redundant steam locomotives dumped in Leen Valley sidings in the mid-1960s. This engine in particular met its fate at Wm. Rigley's yard on Bulwell Common in the Autumn of 1964.
Photo: M.S. Castledine

at Rigleys are said to have witnessed mechanically perfect steam locomotives arrive only to be immobilized by the crew who would jump on a bus back to Colwick, Annesley or wherever they had brought the locos from.

Events followed a woefully predictable pattern once the British economy had irreversibly committed itself to becoming oil-dependent. The Middle East sheiks decided to put the price of oil up! Not just once but several times it shot up with the producers justifying their actions by pointing out that they were doing the West in general and Great Britain in particular a favour by making people aware of the true value of oil.

The formation of the Organisation of Oil Exporting Countries (OPEC) to control producer prices was a very important development in global fuel markets.

Although it didn't help the thousands of British coalminers who had been thrown out of work at the expense of the once cheap oil it did at least expose the shortsightedness of 1960s' political thinking.

Mansfield tended to be central to the Notts coalfield and Berry Hill Park for years hosted major mining carnivals and galas. Hundreds of pitmen from throughout the county used to march with their respective colliery banners through the streets of the town preceded by NUM leaders and political figures of the day. This scene dating from about 1970 shows a front row line-up including left to right George Cheshire, Joe Whelan, Joe Gormley (NUM national president), Len Clarke, Eric Varley (then Labour's energy mister) Len Martin and Don Concannon, MP for Mansfield.
Photo: Mansfield Chronicle Advertiser

Since many railway lines had already been shut under the Tory Government's 'Beeching' regime of 1963 onwards more goods and services were being forced onto the roads but because most vehicles used Middle East oil products including petrol and diesel fuel prices rocketed too as a result of the Arab/Israeli crisis which threatened fuel supplies. A national speed limit was imposed aimed particularly at motorway traffic. The limit of 55mph was later relaxed to 70mph but has never been lifted. The speed limit was designed to conserve fuel by encouraging drivers to travel more slowly.

By the early seventies Britain had a severe case of egg on its face as far as energy policy was concerned and the State had no choice but to reverse its earlier stampede away from coal and into the arms of oil. Pitmen, now realizing that they had become vital pawns in what had by now become a giant international energy powerplay, joined two long and damaging strikes for improved wages and conditions. The first came in 1972 followed by another in 1974 which ended up bringing down Edward Heath's then Conservative Government.

Miners argued that what was good for the Middle East sheiks was good for them. They put their prices up too, and the incoming Labour Government had to cough up the cash for the nouveau riche mineworkers.

So the new Labour regime of 1974 promised a fresh start for Britain and a proper deal for the pits. No more underpaid workers, no more threats from overseas energy supplies and certainly no more mass pit closures. There was a great deal of rhetoric about the need to invest in the pits and to preserve the nation's energy resources.

Back in the Leen Valley the storm of the late 1960s and early 1970s had largely bypassed the district whose pits survived intact save for the closure of Bestwood, which suffered huge financial losses. It was back to business as usual with the bulk of the local pits sending their output to the coal-fired Trent Valley power stations. Mineworkers and their families, encouraged by vastly improved wages and conditions, settled down to the idea of modest affluence with a car in the garage and a colour telly in the lounge; the seventies was the decade when such things made the transition from being regarded as luxury items to everyday chattels. Many Leen Valley pits took in workmen who had transferred from less-fortunate coalfields. Meanwhile the National Coal Board introduced attractive apprenticeship schemes for young men wishing to make a career in coalmining. These schemes were upheld as being among the finest in British industry.

But the 'long life' Leen Valley pits were destined to be an illusory grail. In some coalfields, notably Yorkshire, the 'peace' in the pits between 1974 and 1984 was an uneasy one and in that year fresh unrest led to another round of industrial action and, finally, another proposed national strike.

However this time instead of a direct confrontation between the miners and the NCB or even the Government the powerful National Union of Mineworkers led by its President Arthur Scargill found itself in the disquieting position of having a split within its own ranks. In effect the NUM, once the all-powerful breaker of governments, was going into battle with its own ranks broken before scarcely a shot had been fired.

This came about because many men in the Nottinghamshire coalfield — and in the Leen Valley in particular — disagreed with their own union's tactics and in particular their own leadership's refusal to hold a strike ballot. The upshot was that when the strike call came many Notts. men carried on working. The result of this was an astonishing battle within the ranks of the NUM which ended up with the formation of what amounted to a new breakaway Union of Democratic Mineworkers, after the strike finished, based in Mansfield. The result of a Nottinghamshire ballot was against a strike as it was in all coalfields which voted at that time, including Derbyshire and Wales. The new UDM even took over the former NUM headquarters in Berry Hill forcing the NUM camp to move downmarket into some cramped offices elsewhere in the town.

Meanwhile there had been violent scenes at the district pits.

In the first place acrimony and bad feelings arose in some mining communities where fathers chose to work and sons to strike or vice versa. Many family feuds had their roots in the 1984 dispute and for some the unpleasantness went on for years after the dispute had passed out of the news.

To add fuel to local bitterness some Yorkshire miners — popularly referred to at the time as 'Flying Pickets' — had descended on the district's mines in dawn raids in an effort to persuade men to turn back and go home. Angry scenes developed as hundreds of men pushed, shoved, jostled, shouted and swore around smoking coal braziers outside pit gates. The flying pickets were only concerned with trying to persuade still-working local miners to strike with them. But the local men remained, for the most part, unsympathetic. A few, however, did stay away from work if only to avoid getting involved in any trouble.

As it was, large drafts of police were moved in from all parts of the country to try and foil the movements of these pickets. The police monitored local junctions on the M1 as a matter of course and all vehicles approaching coal towns from the Yorkshire directions were challenged — especially if they were coaches or mini buses!

The effect was to give pit villages like Newstead a kind of civil war atmosphere . . . but in the end and unlike in 1974 the mineworkers were denied any clear victory and there was certainly no fall of government. However the miners who had defied the strike call in Nottinghamshire and elsewhere throughout the Midlands were hailed as heroes by the Prime Minister, Margaret Thatcher. It was Nottinghamshire's resistance to the strike, it was said, that saved Britain from a power crisis (although good coal stocks had undoubtedly helped).

Privately, of course, the Conservatives were delighted to see the once-powerful NUM with its back broken. The Tories were still smarting from the melee of 1974 and were now in a position to deliver retribution. Or so it seemed. It might have been pure coincidence, of course, but after 1985 the British mining industry in the Leen Valley went into rapid decline. This time the Leen Valley pits were not so lucky. Whether the pits had suddenly 'lost' those long term reserves or whether — as is often suggested — the Tories were determined to exact vengeance on all mining communities to settle old scores remains a matter for debate.

Considering what permanent fixtures the pits had been on the district map it seems all the more remarkable that the industry vanished so suddenly and dramatically in the space of some five years. It all happened in the years between 1985 and 1990 give or take a year. These were the years of the demolition men. If the 1970s can be said to have been unsettled for the valley coalmines then the 1980s were nothing short of a catastrophe.

The axe was swung and the district's pits disappeared with astonishing speed. In the period mentioned the Leen Valley coalfield to all intents and purposes ceased to exist . . . only the site at Annesley retained any suggestion of coalmining buildings and this because the former Annesley Colliery merged with Bentinck before being sold to private enterprise. And Calverton, after a period in mothballs, finally re-opened under the control of RJB Mining.

With the pits went many thousands of jobs though lots more were put in jeopardy in local support industries. Many miners, faced with the prospect of their pit closing down, were moved to support protest gestures. However the offer of generous payoffs by the NCB (or British Coal as it became self-styled) served to muffle such protests. The majority of men decided to hang up their lamps quietly and walk

Hucknall Colliery No. 1. As coal mining operations intensified in the Leen Valley district, huge spoil tips were created and much former farmland vanished under these man made heaps of rock and rubble. Aerial ropeways were commonly used to dispose of the waste materials and were a familiar sight at the mines. The creation of a spoil tip is excellently portrayed here at Hucknall No. 1 the surface buildings of which can be seen centre right. Beyond are fields and trees that escaped being tipped upon.... only to be built over instead to create the Ruffs Farm housing estate!
Photo: Notts County Council Leisure Services

away when presented with a 'handshake' of up to £40,000. (In 1985 terms the equivalent of about three years' wages depending on the type of work.)

Such substantial lump sums were conditional upon men agreeing to the redundancy terms promptly and without fuss. Once again there was a suggestion of sudden urgency to slim down the coal-mining industry, only this time it was the Leen Valley pits that were being slimmed down, to employ a classic understatement.

Not only was there a mission to cut out the coalmines, seemingly, but there was a determination to remove all traces of the collieries once they had ceased production. Whether this was a state dictate or just the Coal Board wanting to tidy up after itself will probably never be known but it is interesting to reflect on the thoroughness of the last rites of coal in the Leen Valley. Of course there was considerable incentive to create new spaces for alternative industries or housing on the sites of the old collieries. Some of these initiatives have been more successful than others; the Phoenix Business Park on the site of the Babbington Colliery looks promising . . . but at Hucknall Colliery 10 years after mining ceased there are only a couple of retail outlets amid the wasteland.

When pits closed in earlier decades (say in the Ripley, Ilkeston, Heanor districts) they were often just left alone to decay quietly for some years while fulfilling a sedentary function like ventilating or

A turn-of-the-century demonstration and exhibition by a mines rescue team at Hucknall. Photo: Nottinghamshire County Council Leisure Services.

draining a neighbouring still-working pit sometimes several miles away. Such closed colliery situations were dotted about all over the countryside throughout the first half of the 20th century.

Quaint, home-made looking headstocks could be seen hiding about the countryside usually kept company by a modest collection of tumbledown buildings. A careful observer might also see the former thread of land occupied by a mineral railway. Such backwaters were common well into the 1950s and a lot still survived into the 1960s though these relics of undoubted industrial archaeological value were swept away in the 1970s.

Ilkeston, Pinxton, Eastwood, South Normanton . . . wherever you went outside the Leen Valley the remains of coalmining lay about almost as if abandoned to time.

There WERE some parallels in the Leen Valley but not many by comparison with the Erewash Valley which had had a much longer history of coal workings. Watnall Colliery, for example, had been one of the star pits of the old Barber, Walker Company based at Eastwood. It just scraped into a state ownership situation but closed soon after in 1950.

Watnall was an isolated place for a coalmine midway between Hucknall and Eastwood although for most of its life the mine was dominated by the colossal chimneys of the Watnall brickworks, four of which still survived at this time of writing.

After closure Watnall remained active as a satellite for Moorgreen Colliery the surface buildings there surviving for some 20 years after coal turning ceased. In its final years Watnall's lonely vigil high up on the western flank of the Leen Valley ridge was relieved by the coming of the London-Yorkshire M1 which ran right alongside the colliery yard. Drivers would notice a small concrete headgear and a rather diminutive winding engine house as they travelled the motorway. In its heyday Watnall posessed a tandem headgear made of wood very similar to the one preserved at nearby Brinsley.

Author D H Lawrence mentioned Watnall pit in his book *Sons and Lovers* though it is disguised as 'Nuthall' colliery and High Park is given the pen-name 'Spinney Park'. In any case both were important local pits at the turn of the last century.

Hucknall (No 1) Colliery used to stand on land between the by-pass road and the fire station in Watnall Road and for years after its closure in the early fifties the surface buildings and headgear stood sentry duty overlooking Ruffs housing estate. The steel headframes here looked very much the handiwork of someone with a Meccano set and access to some outsize pram wheels. Long after it ceased producing coal Hucknall's Top Pit acted as a satellite for Babbington.

But in the 1980s round of pit closures there was no such lingering end for the one time 'big hitters' as the National Coal Board used to refer to its star turns like Linby, Hucknall and Newstead. The demolition crews were poised even as the last few tons of coal were drawn up the shafts. Their brief was simple: Fill the shafts, cap the shafts, demolish the surface plant and buildings . . . then level the site. Remove all traces of coal mining.

One thing that proved impossible to remove, however, was the spoil tip at each colliery. You can disguise a tip, re-contour it, plant trees on it and stand on top and admire the view around you but it would cost a lot of money to put it all back!

Some interesting uses have been found for old tips and some even more bizarre ones suggested. In the *Nottingham Evening Post* in February 1996 it was reported that a scheme was being considered to turn the old spoil tip at Linby into a cemetery! At Bestwood the former tipping site has already been incorporated into a country park and a set of headstocks and a winding engine house survive in situ while at Hucknall Colliery former colliers among others now play golf on the old tip. But one of the best and most imaginative uses for an old spoil tip has been at Cossall where there is now a dry ski slope!

Initially the intrusion of coalmining activities on the local landscape would not have been particularly dramatic since by the standards of later years the first pits in the district were compact. However the passage of decades eventually changed this and in the post-Second World War Leen Valley the mines were noticeably dominant landmarks. However even in their early days the pits were generally better equipped and more modern than those in the older established coalfields.

In the beginning the valley's coal measures were tapped by hand using a working method known as 'stall and pillar' which, as the term suggests, allowed for natural support of the roof in working areas. But as the pits were geared up for mechanized mining and powerful machinery took over the work of cutting coal, the method of 'longwall' extraction became universally adopted.

In the longwall method coal was cut by a mechanical shearing machine which took strips of coal up to 250 yards long. The face height varied from a mere two or three feet up to eight feet or more depending on the thickness of the coal seam and each 'bite' could cut into the coal up to two feet. Terrific tonnages could be 'got' each week from just one coal face never mind several and it was this high productivity revolution that made it possible for more mines to top a million tons of output each year.

The downside was that the new style of mechanized mining left no provision for any permanent support of the roof. While actually cutting coal the miners and machines at the coal face were supported by heavy duty hydraulic supports. These supports were advanced to keep up with the production area and once this happened the roof behind was left unsupported and consequently collapsed.

Depending on the depth of the workings this roof collapse would be transmitted eventually to the ground above . . . and the 1950s brought a new and unwelcome feature to all coalmining areas. Subsidence damage soon became a major issue in the coalfields and the Leen Valley suffered along with other coalfields. In one case at Hucknall an entire street of houses was wrecked in 1955 and the locality earned itself some undeserved notoriety as a kind of tourist attraction.

This episode, which affected Belvoir Street, was a portent of things to come for with the mining industry under more and more pressure to dig coal faster and more economically the catalogue of reported damage to land and property increased alarmingly to the point where the Coal Board had to increase staff to deal with the processing of compensation claims.

Subsidence didn't just affect houses. Sometimes large cracks opened up in gardens where coal extraction was going on directly below. In the countryside farmers found their fields had sunk several feet in places forming unexpected ponds in what had earlier been level ground while pipes and sewers below roads buckled and cracked under the pressure of strata movements. Severe speed restrictions had to be slapped on trains as soon as it was spotted that subsidence was upsetting track alignment.

Tracing the district's coalmining history back to early times can be an absorbing activity although as already mentioned the remains are very thinly spread and field work an be frustrated by the existence of replacement industries or buildings of one sort or another that now occupy former mining sites.

Historians generally agree that the Wollaton area was the scene of the first commercial coalmining operations in the 17th Century. The Willoughby family (later to become the Middletons) had profitable enterprises in the district, lucrative enough to finance the stately Wollaton Hall. The Willoughbys engaged one Huntingdon Beaumont to develop their pits and it is Beaumont who is credited with opening the first 'railway' to carry coal away from the estate towards the River Trent. Even further back there are records of coalmining near Cossall in the 14th Century.

Maps from Victorian times show the location of 'old coal pits' at or about the present day location of Radford Bridge Road and Glaisdale Drive and these are probably the earliest pits to be found within a modest distance of the River Leen and, for that matter, the Nottingham city centre. Any traces of these workings would have vanished under the expanding inner suburbs of the city many years ago.

However, in recognizing the former existence of these sites we can conveniently illustrate how the valley's coalfield splits into two distinct parts which, for simplicity, we can refer to as the upper and lower districts.

And it is in the lower district — Radford, Wollaton, Strelley etc — where we encounter what geologists refer to as the fringes of the 'exposed' coalfield which means an area where the coal seams are very close to the surface or even where they thrust out of the ground in which case they are said to 'outcrop'. In the upper district the coal measures slope away into deeper ground and are therefore said to be 'concealed'. The further east you go the deeper the seams become and eventually they disappear below the bed of the North Sea on their way to mainland Europe.

All the early coalmines on the Nottinghamshire/ Derbyshire border were developed on the exposed coalfield which, roughly speaking, lay to the west of a line drawn from Nottingham to Chesterfield. The primitive working methods available for hundreds

The Babbington Colliery surface layout of 1960 bore little resemblance to the original 1844 Thomas North venture except for the presence of the tandem headgear in the centre of the picture. These were the 'windy' and 'smokey' shafts of furnace ventilation days and amazingly they remained in use right until the end, albeit using modern electrically powered equipment. Note also the 'traffic density' on the A610 nearly four decades ago!

of years up to the mid 19th century meant that only shallow seams could be worked. So-called 'Bell pits' were very common throughout the Middle Ages and later.

By contrast the upper district consisted of 'modern' collieries properly financed and opened out that were much deeper than those in the lower district so that hitherto unreachable reserves could be tapped. Unlike the simple pits of the exposed coalfield the new ventures were set up right from the start to be profitable as well as prolific producers, although there always remained an element of gambling in coalmining. By Victorian standards the new sinkings had 'state-of-the-art' trimmings like powerful steam winding engines to haul the coal up the shafts. Earlier efforts relied on horse or even hand windlass power.

No study of the Leen Valley coal industry could start anywhere else but with Thomas North.

Although a name lost on present citizens of Basford and district, North, who was once Lord Mayor of Nottingham, played a very important role in the early days of the upper district and he, more than anyone else, deserves the title of founder of the valley coalfield.

It was in 1843 when North, at the time a modestly successful coal owner, opened the new Babbington Colliery which, for its time, was a thoroughly modern affair with tremendous potential. How tremendous North would never know for the venture struggled to begin with and did not really become profitable for several years. In the end Babbington had a long and illustrious history and, until its closure in 1987, it had the distinction of being the oldest pit then working in the Nottinghamshire coalfield.

North was also responsible for other sinkings at Whitemoor (Newcastle Colliery) and Bulwell in 1853 and 1867 respectively. In fact the 1860s and 1870s appears to have been something of a hectic period for sinkings since most of the rest of the upper district pits were established at this time. Wollaton and Clifton in the lower district saw two new mines open in the second half of the 19th century while Radford was sunk as a satellite of Wollaton just before the turn of the century.

It was said of Thomas North after his death in 1868, aged 57, that 'by his great enterprise he was the means of finding employment for a large number of people' and these are exactly the words on a memorial to him in Old Basford churchyard.

In partnership with two other men — Thomas Wakefield and James Morley — North set about his new project at Babbington with great enthusiasm though he clearly underestimated the tremendous drain on capital that would occur before the new mine would turn the corner of profitability.

Throughout its long life Babbington Colliery had the confusing problem of also being known as the Cinderhill Colliery. This was bad enough for strangers to the area but to compound matters one of North's earlier pits was also called Babbington and reasonably so because it WAS at Babbington, a small hamlet between Kimberley and Ilkeston which still survives today. This confusion needn't trouble the present day student unduly for the old and original Babbington pit is thought to have closed down as long ago as 1860 just as the new Leen Valley pits were being developed.

At the time of its sinking the new Babbington Colliery was well out in open country to the west of Nottingham and looked to Basford or Bulwell for its workforce. But in later years it was encroached upon by an ever-expanding Nottingham suburbia and in the final decades was in close proximity to the sizable Bells Lane housing estate scheme. The surface plant at Babbington was a distinctive landmark for motorists arriving at or leaving the city via the A610 road and the site was within a mile of the M1.

Money to finance North's new venture came not only out of his own pocket but also from the partners and, of course, his existing pits were able to contribute some of their profits to the new mine. As we have already noted, however, the colliery took a lot of supporting financially and although money was freely available to begin with this state of affairs couldn't last indefinitely especially since at this time the coal trade was experiencing something of a depression anyway.

What coal was produced at Babbington in the early days was sold for ready cash. The partnership was anxious to see a reversal in the one-way flow of funds! So while the new colliery was something of a sight to behold for the locals as well as being a feather in Nottingham area's industrial cap, behind the scenes, finances were running on something of a knife edge. North was forced to borrow heavily to see the project completed but sadly he died, heavily in debt before the corner was turned.

The colliery and other assets were seized by North's bankers and, ironically, not long after his death there was a revival in the coal trade and the early 1870s were boom times for coalowners. Had North survived a year or two longer he would probably have rejoiced in paying back all the money he owed . . . and possibly enjoyed a comfortable retirement.

North had been unlucky. With the benefit of hindsight it is clear that he was not a bad mining engineer nor was he an unwise investor.

He just did the right things but at the wrong time and overstretched his credit lines into the bargain. It would probably be fairer to regard Thomas North as a man of considerable vision and ability; someone who not only pioneered one of the valley's first modern early coal-mines but also introduced the then novel concept of providing housing for his workers and their families, not to mention his unique private standard gauge railway system linking his pits to the Nottingham Canal at Radford.

To the people who worked for him North was something of a hero, a fact borne out by the crowds who turned out to pay their last respects as his funeral procession made its way through the Basford streets. Many saw him as a true local benefactor for Old Basford had been a poor framework knitting village prior to the arrival of the new mine and North offered young men the alternative of much better paid work. Many went on to rent substantial dwellings from the coalowner. Some of them were furnished with sizable allotments or good-sized gardens so that pitmen could grow their own food.

Shaft sinking, however expensive, was something that Thomas North evidently had a passion for. The original shafts that he put down at Babbington in 1843 remained in use for the pit's entire life and even had names (Windy and Smokey) harking back to the days of furnace ventilation. But at seven feet wide they did restrict the flow of materials and coal and some observers have expressed surprise that he didn't develop Babbington with wider diameter shafts.

In 1855 he sought fresh opportunities and began a series of sinkings in the neighbourhood and once again new shafts were seven feet wide. Ten years after the opening of Babbington two more shafts were put down to the Top Hard seam at Whitemoor in a venture that became known as Newcastle Colliery after the Duke of Newcastle upon whose land it was built. Although coal turning ceased here as long ago as 1928 (making it possibly the first Leen Valley pit to close) the site was retained as a coal wharf well into the 1960's.

There was another foray at Broxtowe but then came further shafts at Babbington itself to relieve pressure on the existing limited shaft capacity. Known as the Hempshill shaft project this was also intended to help with ventilation. Later yet another 10-foot diameter shaft was opened nearby.

Shortly after North's death yet another shaft was put down this time at Bulwell little more than a mile away from Babbington. It was originally known as No. 5 but from 1877 to 1945 enjoyed the somewhat more dignified title of Bulwell Colliery. Although a small affair and not really typical of the mainstream Leen Valley pits Bulwell did, evidently, have a character all of its own and enjoyed an unsurpassed reputation for the quality of its housecoal. Even now old folk in and around Bulwell talk affectionately of 'Shonkey' pit. The nickname derived from the pit's haulage engine which was an upended locomotive.

Author Claude Bartholomew in his book *The Leen Valley* gives a fascinating personal account of an underground visit to Bulwell Colliery one Sunday morning in 1936. He wrote that while descending the shaft the sound of falling water was clearly audible. At the end of the visit the author was told that the term 'Shonkey' arose from the tendency of this unconventional engine to dance about on its mountings when working at full speed!

So far we have learned that coalmining in the lower district took place at a much earlier date than even Thomas North's venture but it is fair to say that North was the first local entrepreneur to properly attempt the commercial extraction of coal with the sinking of his Babbington Colliery. That he and his partners were almost continuously beset by financial headaches was unfortunate but does

Hucknall Colliery in Portland Road was styled No. 2 to avoid confusion with the Watnall Road pit, No. 1. After wholesale rebuilding in the 1950s and 1960s, the Portland Road facilities dominated the lower part of the town and the colossal headstocks (left) serving the Blackshale seam competed with the parish church of St. Mary Magdalene! Inset: Hucknall Portland Road Colliery as it looked circa 1890.

not detract from the significance of the new 'winning' on the historical map.

North was not only a businessman who happened to turn to coal but he was also a kind of philanthropist as well in as much as he tried his best to retain and house his workmen and their families. In the 1850s a job with Thomas North was no doubt a sought-after career for fit young men in the Basford, Bulwell and Whitemoor districts.

The little group of pits that North and his partners ran, Babbington, Hempshill, Newcastle and Bulwell, were not to be on their own for long for by the end of the 1860s other entrepeneurs were moving in on the upper district. By 1869, for example, Hucknall had joined the coal age and had a pit in Portland Road alongside the Nottingham to Mansfield railway line and another to the west of the town a mile up Watnall Road both sunk by Ellis and Company while W. Worswick's Annesley mine had also come into production during the 1860s.

Barber, Walker & Company's new sinking at Watnall on the valley's western flank was also turning coal by now while shortly after the turn of the 1870s the coal boom took off in earnest. First came Clifton Colliery on the banks of the River Trent close to its confluence with the Leen, Bestwood Collliery was developed in 1871/72, Linby mine arrived amid the fields at about the same time followed quickly by sinkings at Wollaton and then Newstead.

This headlong procession of sinkings wasn't just a local phenomenon . . . it was going on at much the same rate in other coalfields. For example the number of mines operating in 1869 was around 2,782 but within just SIX years this number had all but doubled! Not all new coalmining ventures were on the same scale as the big, new, Leen Valley sinkings but it does, nevertheless, give some indication of the buoyancy of coal's growth as a major UK industry in Victorian England.

To give some idea of the escalating national demand for coal an average of some 70,000,000 tons was being won each year in the late 1850s and early 1860s. The figure was 105,000,000 a decade later. There was an equally impressive upward trend in mining employment opportunities in Notts between 1874 and 1920 when the number of workmen employed underground shot up from around 9,000 to nearly 42,000. There was also a fourfold increase in the total number of men in mining jobs both above and below. Even boys living in villages like Basford, where other, cleaner, non-mining jobs could be had, preferred the enhanced wages obtainable from pitwork.

And word soon spread. Pay, traditionally better in coalmining towns than in poorer agricultural districts, continued to tempt fresh recruits into the industry and it has been said that pay rates were so attractive as to draw farm labourers from as far away as the South of England. It would be interesting to learn if any modern residents in the Leen Valley with former coalmining associations have been able to trace their ancestry back to such migrations.

In his book *Mining in the East Midlands 1550-1947* published in 1971, Dr Alan Griffin notes that the Leen Valley pits had the advantage of thick seams of Top Hard coal to exploit. He points out that they were technologically modern and their workings were initially close to their respective pit bottoms. Coalowners tended to jack up output in depressed years in order to keep profits up. But this tactic also served to depress prices. This led the General Manager of the Barber, Walker Company in 1887 to lament on the prices for coal from his pits being driven down to their lowest level for years. The implication in this observation was that the Leen Valley coalfield was to blame for coal from his pits being driven down to their lowest level for years. The implication in this observation was that the Leen Valley coalfield was to blame for over production.

Annesley Colliery is the only remaining site of active coal mining in the Leen Valley, although no coal actually surfaces here any longer. This mine has had a chequered career and even under private enterprise in the 1990s continues to be beset by financial difficulties. The shafts here were the deepest of any of the district's mines.
Photo: Ray Mills

In retrospect it seems odd that the Barber, Walker Company with pits so close to the Leen Valley district failed to involve itself more here although as we shall see in a moment there was one slight glimmer. As it was they stuck to their sites at Moorgreen, High Park, Watnall and elsewhere.

The new pits had something of a head start over their mainly older competitors just across the Misk Hills and we learn from Dr Griffin's work that even in the coal slump of the 1880's the new Leen Valley sinkings coped while other more shaky concerns over the border in Derbyshire struggled and, in some cases, shut altogether.

An exception to this generalization was at Annesley Colliery. The valley's most northerly sinking had a somewhat chequered career even in its early days, suffering from under investment and just plain old fashioned bad luck. The Worswick family moved from Leicestershire and decided to plough what capital they had from their old pits at Colerton and Swannington into Annesley's development. The Worswicks also took a financial interest in the sinking at Linby a mile or so down the valley towards Hucknall.

The under capitalization of Annesley was doubtless a reflection on the relatively short lease available on the coal seam here. In modern parlance the Worswicks perhaps took the view that they were only interested in a quick return on cash invested; a quick killing. At one point the Barber, Walker Company WERE offered the Annesley lease but decided against taking it up and in the end Annesley was taken over by the Hardwick Colliery Company in 1904. Even the new owners didn't persevere for by 1924 the mine once again changed hands this time with the New Hucknall Colliery Company assuming control. This company reportedly had to invest heavily to reverse years of neglect and underfunding.

Paradoxically in the post-nationalization years of the late 20th century Annesley/Bentinck (as it is now termed) continues to be harried by financial obstacles. In spite of its unfortunate reputation, however, this pit remained the valley's last outpost of coalmining.

As an independent unit Annesley continued to surface and wash coal until the end of the 1960s but by this time the Top Hard had been worked out and the output came from the Deep Soft seam. The coal-raising shaft, or 'downcast' shaft was the more easterly of the two pits and was one of the deepest in the coalfield. Not surprisingly a substantial steam winding engine was needed to haul minecars from pit bottom about a third of a mile below ground.

The tremendous machine that operated here was dismantled in about 1968 to make way for an electrically-powered winding engine

Wollaton Colliery was a low profile mine that carried out its work without too much disturbance to the local community. This mine died quietly in the mid 1960s and the site is now occupied by executive houses. Note the canal lock gates.

Radford Colliery, unlike other Leen Valley pits, had plenty of competition for labour. Major factories like Raleigh and Players had to draw from the same 'pool' of workers as did the mine. There was little fear of 'unemployment' in those days, in fact the word was not in the local vocabulary!

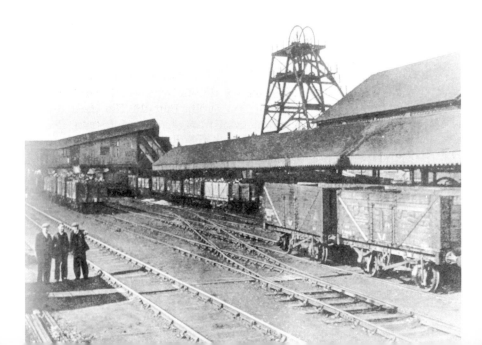

but until this happened the raising of coal from Annesley's shaft was something that could easily be witnessed by an observer on Dorket Head above Arnold. On any clear day a towering column of white steam was visible as it billowed out of the engine's exhaust below Robin Hood Hills.

We have already seen that a mine opened at Wollaton in the Nottingham suburbs in the mid 1870s and the company behind this venture was styled Wollaton Collieries Ltd. It might be that the plural form implied further expansion and in fact this did happen but not for more than 29 years. The expansion emerged as Radford Colliery as late as 1897.

Despite a proliferation of smaller pits in this part of the coalfield in earlier times there was still plenty of coal to go for — particularly so in the relatively untouched Deep Hard seam. Although some mining historians argue that Wollaton was not strictly speaking a Leen Valley pit there can be no such doubt about Radford because the river flowed past the pit entrance gates!

Both Wollaton and Radford, although their sinkings were separated by 23 years, were planned to yield 400 tons of coal daily each. Unlike their more northerly counterpart at Annesley these two small pits had a relatively trouble-free and low-profile life. In fact both Wollaton and Radford enjoyed long and steady careers though they never aspired to the million-ton-a-year-league reputation of some near neighbours.

Output from both units probably peaked in about 1910 when, working as a combine, daily output hit a commendable 2,600 tons. At this time the overall manpower was about 1,800. It should be remembered, of course, that this level of production was BEFORE the introduction of the mechanisation era. The coal was all 'hand got'. Nor should the size of the workforce of pre-First World War Wollaton/Radford go unremarked. A firm today that employed some 2,000 personnel would be rated as a major local player.

By the close of the Second World War the combine was run down and just 750 men were struggling to achieve 1,000 tons weekly. Radford, in particular, suffered from competition for labour. Unlike most of the rest of the Leen Valley pits this mine was surrounded by alternative and attractive employment opportunities.

The world-famous Raleigh cycle works was within the parish and not far away another global company, Players, looked to their own doorstep for workers. So too did a scattering of bleachers, brewers, soap makers and so on.

But for men who chose to adopt coalmining as a career, as many did, working conditions here were always comfortable and the air quality both in the Wollaton and Radford workings was always said to be good and dry with no gas present. Indeed some workmen are reported to have provided their own candle and worked by naked light . . . though whether this would have been tolerated upon nationalization seems doubtful.

We noted earlier how the National Coal Board invested heavily in some of the upper mines. But money needed investing everywhere from top to bottom of the coalfield not only in the interests of modernization but also to rectify the rundown of the war years. At Radford, for example, the NCB installed a trunk belt system of conveyors and five Samson longwall coalcutters were allocated to each pit and, by 1950, there was the promise of pithead baths.

Most intriguing of all, however, was the plan to uprate underground ventilation by scrapping the old steam-driven aeroplane propeller and replacing it with an electrically-driven one. It is tempting to wonder how an aeroplane propeller ended up at Radford Colliery in the first place . . . unless some long-forgotten mechanical engineer had been on good terms with somebody at Hucknall Aerodrome in days gone by.

Most of the spending on Wollaton/Radford was directed towards underground improvements and general modernization and certainly the money seemed to have been well spent for by the beginning of the 1950s the combine was back in the pink with a daily output of 2,150 tons. Productivity, climbed from 26cwts to 40cwts per man shift.

Statistical and mechanical data aside it should never be forgotten that collieries were places of immense social and community importance. Radford mine may have been unusual in having many other industries on its doorstep but in the main the local pit was THE big and often ONLY source of employment. Workmen who gave half a century of service — and often more — to the mining industry were commonplace and in the pre-television era collieries all had their quota of characters or individuals who put their own stamp on the working day.

Radford Colliery had bachelor Bill Elkington, for half a century an employee looking after pit ponies there. But with the introduction of the trunk belt system of conveyors by the NCB his job was becoming redundant. Bill's routine every morning, seven days a week, was to arise at 3.45am, leave his house in nearby Peter Street and set off for work. Down the pit he knew all the animals by name (Winston, Eden, Bevin and so on) and *they* recognized his approaching footsteps underground.

After attending to the animals Bill returned to the surface for 'lunch' at around 8am, potter in his garden for a while and then go back to the pit again until 5pm. He retired to bed, promptly at 9pm!

Another Radford favourite was resident mouser 'Ginger' the tomcat who was also looked after by Bill Elkington. Ginger lived underground like the ponies and had been born below ground and spent his entire 14 year career patrolling the miles of passageways and tunnels below Wollaton and Radford. He was once taken to the surface when a kitten but elected to go back down again!

The reader should bear in mind that at the time of its sinking Radford Colliery was on the extreme western fringe of the city while Wollaton mine was well out in open country although not too far away from the small village from which it took its name. In some respects it is interesting to contrast Wollaton's physical situation with that of, say, Linby. Both were relatively small and otherwise unspoiled villages that suddenly had coalmines open up in their immediate backyards.

In both cases while the industrial intrusion came close it did manage just to remain out of the immediate view. Like Linby, Wollaton did not attach itself to the pit in terms of providing housing and labour and so neither had to absorb any of the mining community infrastructure that was forced upon villages elsewhere as at Bestwood, Hucknall and, in particular, Calverton where the original farming village had to brace itself to absorb hundreds of new arrivals as mineworkers — with their families — moved in to take jobs at the new mine on the outskirts of the village. A new and substantial housing estate was built at Calverton specifically for the village's newly-arrived workforce.

Linby village remained aloof to the closure of the nearby mine in 1988 and by the time of Wollaton mine's closure in the mid 1960s the original village had long since been surrounded by commuter suburbia. Interestingly the presence of a coalmine in the parish didn't stop Wollaton gaining the reputation of being an affluent district sought after by people seeking an address in one of the city's nicer backwaters, for as coalmines went, the one at Wollaton pursued its business in a low-profile way and managed to avoid creating a skyscraping spoil hill.

Doubtless there are people now living in Wollaton who have no idea there ever was a coalmine in the village. A housing development occupies the site of the former industry. And again to contrast Wollaton with Linby it is interesting to see that residential housing and industrial units have replaced the former mine buildings.

However much rebuilding and modernization was to take place in the valley's pits the most dramatic development to affect the coalfield was the opening out of the new mine at Calverton. This is sometimes, and mistakenly, thought of as a major post-war NCB project . . . but in fact Calverton Colliery was first conceived and site work started in the late 1930s by Bestwood Associated Collieries Ltd the Chairman and Managing Director of which said that but for the intervention of the Second World War the mine would almost certainly have been completed and in production by 1947, the year of nationalization.

But the war did intervene and the newly created NCB inherited the task of opening out Calverton and bringing the pit into production and not without considerable international publicity since the new project was resulting in the creation of one of the most technologically modern deep coalmines in the world.

Calverton's Number 1 shaft had already been sunk by 1940 and a number of surface buildings erected. Development work on Number 2 shaft began in January 1946 and was continued throughout that year by Bestwood Associated Collieries Ltd who had already decided to adopt the strata freezing method in order to contain a serious water problem earlier encountered while sinking the first shaft.

What followed was nothing short of an engineering marvel.

The sinking of Calverton's shafts was an epic of mining engineering that captured worldwide attention and during operations mining engineers from as far away as the United States of America travelled to Nottinghamshire to view progress. In sinking the first shaft workmen had encountered colossal amounts of water leaking into the workings from the porous red sandstone. As much as 1,000 gallons a minute had been pumped to the surface. To stem this inrush during the sinking of Number 2, holes were bored down through the sandstone, pipes run into them and then, with the assistance of a surface refrigeration plant, a wall of ice was built up through which the second shaft could be cut.

The principle was not entirely new since earlier sinkings in this country had used strata freezing techniques. It was the scale of its usage at Calverton and the type of geology encountered that set this project apart from others.

The sinkers, wearing special thermal clothing to protect them from the arctic conditions in the freezing shaft, reached their first goal (the High Main seam) which was just a yard thick and the High Main 'horizon' was established as a first pit bottom with the intention of later dropping it to the Low Hazel seam to serve output from coal faces in the Main Bright and High Hazel seams.

No doubt Thomas North would have been greatly impressed by Calverton had he been around to see it for himself. Coalmining technology had advanced by a century since North's heyday when Babbington Colliery was the last word in the then contemporary coalmining scene. North probably knew or at least suspected the presence of abundant coal measures to the east of Nottingham where

Sinkers about to be hauled up the shaft during the opening out of Calverton Colliery in about 1947.

no coal workings had previously existed. But there was no way that mid-19th century sinking technology could have coped with the problems encountered at Calverton.

In Thomas North's day coalmining was only just emerging from largely medieval methods of working into early technology . . . and it was thanks to people like him that it did so.

Mining engineers from around the world came to Nottinghamshire to observe the opening out of Calverton Colliery in the late 1940s. Calverton sinkers had to use a special technique to freeze the strata to prevent inrushes of water from the local sandstone.

ROLLS ROYCE LTD.

IN THE CLOSING YEARS of the First World War the upper Leen Valley became host to 'Those Magnificent Men in their Flying Machines' as the recently-formed Royal Air Force established Hucknall Aerodrome in fields on the left-hand side of Watnall Road. Built in November 1917, the site officially 'opened' for business on 1 April, 1918 . . . on the same day as the RAF was formed under Lord Trenchard.

Curiously the rather outdated term 'Aerodrome' stuck long after it had gone out of use everywhere else so that even in modern times the phrase is still acceptable vocabulary in the district.

The Royal Air Force's tenure at Hucknall ended many years ago after a long and distinguished run during which townfolk became used to seeing many famous aircraft types in the local skies.

But the RAF's presence in the upper Leen Valley, though highly interesting and exciting particularly to aircraft buffs, was eclipsed by the arrival of Rolls Royce in late 1934.

It is important that this distinction is made early for the Hucknall site had, and still has in Rolls Royce's case, what might be termed a split role in the historical record.

During the later 1930s and into the years of the Second World War there was a tremendous expansion of the RAF almost entirely brought about by the needs of the war effort and airfields or aerodromes were established at many locations in the East Midlands. For example an 'emergency' landing ground was identified on Papplewick Moor of all places though it is thought this was only used on one occasion when an aircraft was forced down there and the crew, luckily, escaped and made their way to the nearby Griffin's Head.

Another airfield was created not far away on high ground near Longdale Lane at Blidworth and this did for a time see activity. The mess buildings are now part of the Longdale Rural Craft Centre.

And, of course, further east dozens of bomber stations were established — a few of them still in Nottinghamshire but the vast majority spreading into Lincolnshire, Yorkshire and Cambridgeshire.

Such bases have rapidly vanished from the countryside in most cases although in doing so have generated an enormous amount of interest leading to the publication of some fascinating books avidly snapped up by those who take an interest in vintage wartime aircraft matters.

Hucknall Aerodrome might well have vanished from the local scene, too, and we have Rolls Royce to thank for an unintentional act of salvation. For in adopting Hucknall as its base for flight development and engine research the airfield was not only saved for posterity but became linked with some of the world's most advanced pioneering work.

Hucknall Aerodrome, therefore, has two 'histories' on the one site. First came the RAF and later Rolls Royce, the latter assuming such local importance since it provided 'civilian' employment to so many Leen Valley people.

Since much of our look at Hucknall's golden days of aviation will centre around the considerable achievements of Rolls Royce we will start by taking a brief look at the aerodrome's early RAF days. It appears that Papplewick Moor was, in fact, considered early on as a permanent runway although the ground was found to be too waterlogged and the present site adopted . . . though as already noted the Papplewick location did eventually become a reserve landing area.

Land was purchased at Watnall Road, Westville, from the Duke of Portland and a firm of contractors from Blackpool was appointed to undertake construction work which included ample take-off and landing facilities, hangars and associated buildings.

It appears, however, that Hucknall was a training ground rather than an operational station at this period and among pilots who were tutored there were some American flyers in Curtiss Jennies. When

504 Squadron based at RAF Hucknall in the early 1930s
Photo: Stan Grainger/Rolls Royce Heritage

the First World War ended the RAF, surprisingly, decided to abandon their newly-created facilities in the Leen Valley and accordingly the Air Ministry offered the site for sale and some of the buildings, where suitable, were turned into civilian dwellings. A farmer, George Elkington, eventually acquired the entire site comprising 107 acres.

This might well have been the end of the aviation story at Hucknall. But the Air Ministry, in an odd bureaucratic loop-the-loop, decided to buy back the site from farmer Elkington along with additional parcels of land which included Bulwell Hall. There then followed a period of rebuilding and upgrading of the original aerodrome by main contractors Laing and in the Spring of 1928, No 504 (County of Nottingham) Squadron was installed.

No. 504 Squadron was a Special Reserve Unit (Day Bombers) equipped with Hawker Horsleys until 1934 when the squadron re-equipped with Westland Wallaces though by Spring 1937 these, too, had been ousted to make way for the more agile Hawker Hind. Finally, in the autumn of 1938, 504 squadron became a fighter unit and pilots received the RAF's latest combat machine — the eight-gun Hawker Hurricane Mk 1 — and it was with these that the squadron eventually moved out of the Leen Valley to see action initially in France and later back in the British Isles.

Earlier, in the years immediately before the outbreak of the Second World War, another squadron made Hucknall its home. This was 98 Squadron which moved in with its Hawker Hinds. Local folk often became more closely acquainted with these aeroplanes than they expected to, for many crash landed around the district, the autumn of 1937 seeing a spate of such mishaps with planes coming down at Broxtowe, Gunthorpe Bridge and Pinxton!

Another unit arrived at Hucknall with its Hawker Hinds. 104 (Bomber) Squadron had re-formed at Abingdon in the 1930s RAF expansion programme. The squadron came to Hucknall in August 1936 . . . but had moved out again in the early summer of 1938.

By September 1939 and the outbreak of war Hucknall was, therefore, under Fighter Command control — but with no fighter aircraft on its books. Still in residence were crews of 98 Squadron (by

Hucknall 1938. Fairey Battle, Hawker 'Merlin' Horsley, Whitney Straight, Heinkel HE70, High Speed Hawker Fury, Hawker Hart and special Hart with PV12 engine. Left background building is dynamometer engine test bed.
Photo: Stan Grainger/Rolls Royce Heritage

this time equipped with the notoriously ineffective Fairey Battle machines) — but in June this unit moved to Bramcote though they returned the following year this time with a few Tiger Moths on strength to augment the Battles.

However, as can be seen, it served mainly as a 'transit camp' for pilots and aircraft rather than as a front line operational station though throughout the war it continued to operate as an Elementary Flying Training School for Polish flyers under one guise or another. Certainly during the early war years Hucknall's chief contribution to the air war effort (apart from pilot training) was the repair of damaged fighters which was carried out by Rolls Royce who had, for some years, had a rapidly expanding presence at Hucknall.

After the war Hucknall welcomed back its original 504 Squadron by now re-equipped with DeHavilland Mosquito fighter-bombers. But with the 1950s dawned the site's final period as an RAF base. For by 1957 all military flying activity ceased although Rolls Royce flight development testing of its engines continued until 1971. Runway improvements and lengthening had been carried out in the mid-1950s and much of the hardcore for this was moved to the aerodrome from Linby Colliery.

To the general public of the Leen Valley however, Hucknall Aerodrome was almost certainly best remembered for the Empire Air Day displays of the 1930s although as a matter of note air shows continued to take place at Hucknall throughout the 1950s and 1960s although the post-war events were aeroplane spectaculars in their own right rather than government-inspired morale-boosting exercises as the pre-war events had been.

In a letter to the *Hucknall Dispatch* and the *Nottingham Evening Post* Stan Grainger wrote, in October 1994:

"One of the biggest annual events in this area during the 30s was the Empire Air Day at Hucknall aerodrome. In July 1934 the government decided on a massive expansion of the RAF to combat the possible threat from Europe, and the Empire Air Days, at around 40 Air stations, were started as an 'at home' PR exercise to justify the cost and political implications.

The first display at Hucknall was held on 25 May, 1935, when an estimated 3,000 people visited the aerodrome to see the local 504 Squadron hosting many other Royal Air Force attractions. In addition to seeing a varied flying display and viewing aircraft of the day, including the Westland Wallace, Avro training machines, Bolton and Paul Sidestrands, and three Hawker Harts, powered by Rolls Royce 'Kestrel' engines, visitors were allowed to inspect armament, photographic and navigation sections.

Formation flying was highly attractive, and many admired the skill of the pilots in manoeuvring the flight of five planes in a manner as though tied together with string.

By 1939 the number of stations involved in these 'at home' days had increased to 63. Hucknall's attendance reached 'in excess' of 35,000. I say 'in excess' because a portion of the fence broke down and an estimated 2,000 got in without paying. The roads round about were choked with traffic, a Trent bus took one-and-a-half hours to travel from the market to the aerodrome.

One man paid half-a-crown to park his bike in someone's front garden. Sir Kingsley Wood, Secretary of State for Air, flew in a D.H. 91 Albatross, he was received by Air Vice-Marshall T.L. Mallery AOC. No 12 Fighter Group. Particular interest was shown in the state of the art equipment of the day, including the Merlin engine, the appearance of the new, 335mph Hurricane, Fairey Battle and Handley Page Hampden bombers. The highlight of the day was the 'mock' raid on an oil refinery when the battles roared in and played havoc with oil soaked wooden dummy buildings, clouding the airfield in black smoke and stink."

This was all before my time . . . but I could remember the post-war years at Hucknall and the airshows there not to mention the constant comings and goings of all manner of aircraft types. My grandfather had been posted to RAF Hucknall in January 1940 having been moved back to 'home duties' from Egypt. Warrant Officer Frederick M. Weiss MBE arrived in the town fresh from life amid the pyramids and camels to find a drastically different environment in the Leen Valley . . . the nearest thing to pyramids were coal waste tips; even Hucknall aerodrome itself was overshadowed by the surface sprawl of Hucknall No. 1 Colliery in Watnall Road.

In a letter to Stan Grainger I expressed an interest in his memories of flying from Hucknall and promptly received a letter back encouraging me in my work on this book. He wrote: "I will be most delighted to help you with your research wherever I can. I too am also interested in the history of local industry as I was a councillor for 12 years initially with Hucknall Urban District Council and later for Ashfield District Council. Can I suggest that you might like to come and have a look around the Rolls Royce Heritage Centre?"

It is only thanks to the voluntary hard work of a dedicated group of former Rolls Royce employees that the Heritage Centre came into being at Hucknall at all and the collection of historic material — including aero engines — they have assembled is almost certainly unique. But more importantly the small band of enthusiasts who look after the Heritage Centre — once highly skilled men now in retirement — have an asset more important than physical artefacts: their own knowledge, experience and recollections.

On what became one of my regular Wednesday morning visits to the Rolls Royce Heritage Centre during the Spring of 1995 and while preparing this chapter I was fortunate to be introduced to Colin Gibson, a man who had enjoyed a long and interesting career with Rolls Royce and whose father, Ted Gibson, had been one of the company's test engineers.

Colin had already identified the need for someone to put down in writing the highlights of what happened at Hucknall in years past and at this point I would like to thank him for placing at my disposal the results of his own research as well as his late father's recollections. With Colin's helpful gesture I was saved many hours of what would otherwise have been arduous research.

Colin's own career with Rolls Royce Ltd began in November 1940 when as a keen 15-year-old he joined the company as an apprentice and subsequently saw service in just about every department from the drawing office to the flight development section.

His father — full name Taylor Gibson — arrived at the company

by an accident of what might be termed wartime exigency for he had earlier been a coalmining engineer at Seaton Delavell in the Northumberland coalfield!

Taylor Gibson had joined up to fight in the First World War and in due course found himself at Normanton Barracks, Derby, on his way, as he thought, to France with thousands more. This was in 1915. At this time the young Rolls Royce company needed more engineers to help with wartime demands and the fact that Taylor Gibson was a mining engineer didn't stop him being plucked from the crowd to go and learn about aero engines. After all, he was

Colin Gibson 1940

an engineer. In those days the distinction was academic.

During the First World War Taylor Gibson spent a great deal of time working with aircraft engine development on experimental test-beds at Derby, and to his delight the company offered him continuing employment when peace arrived. Hence he had a proper job with the company rather than being seconded from the Army.

In an interview by Martin Stevenson of the Nottingham Evening Post in July 1977, Taylor Gibson gave an interesting insight into the early days of Rolls Royce at Hucknall. In one classic comment he said: "Hucknall Aerodrome was leased (by Rolls Royce) from the Air Ministry in

Taylor (Ted) Gibson joined Rolls Royce in 1915 at Derby, moving to Hucknall in 1934.
Photo: C.T. Gibson

Merlin powered Hawker Horsley with Ted Gibson in the cockpit, circa 1936
Photo: C.T. Gibson

1935. We took over the vacant hangars which were just about falling to pieces and swarming with rats, starlings, pigeons and things — spent about the first week shooting them.

"Temporary repairs were made, offices set up and the place made habitable."

It is worthwhile tracing the Rolls Royce aero engine development story back to the beginning and to before the time Hucknall became involved, for in 1927 the company finally accepted the fact that if it was to progress in this sector of the marketplace it would be necessary to have an in-house flight test and development facility. In other words it was no use the company designing and building engines for aircraft if it had no aircraft in which to fit and test its products.

A first step in this direction was the decision to buy an old First World War DeHavilland DH9a biplane into which was fitted an 'FX' (later Kestrel) engine. The DeHavilland company agreed to service and fly the aircraft from their Hatfield headquarters north of London. While not exactly 'in house' from the Rolls Royce point of view at Derby at least it was a start and first trials took place towards the end of that year when Colin's father occupied the rear cockpit where instrumentation had been fitted to monitor engine performance and conditions.

The result? After 122 flying hours in this somewhat outdated machine valuable research data had been gathered and the company was satisfied that the venture had been well worthwhile although the hapless aeroplane, by this time worn out, was sent for scrap. So the results of these tests had proved beyond any doubt that Rolls Royce were justified in doing their own flight development . . . yet they were still having to rely on others to carry it out for them.

By the early 1930s a more promising move back to the Nottingham area occurred and Rolls Royce occupied a corner of the Nottingham Flying Club's premises at Tollerton. First aircraft to arrive was a Hawker Horsley (J 8001) on 16 September, 1931, from Farnborough. It was fitted with a Buzzard III engine and was engaged on a variety of tests concerning radiators, oilcoolers, vibration, fuel and ignition. And the following week another aircraft type arrived this time a Fairey IIIF (J 9173) powered by a Kestrel II unit. Similar tests were carried out and between them the two machines flew more than 200 hours before they were declared of no further use. Third aircraft to arrive at Tollerton was Hawker Hart (K 2969).

Said Colin: "At this point it was obvious that the work being carried out and the results being achieved at Tollerton were beginning to bear fruit. The company decided that a more permanent home was needed where the aero engine section could have its own self-contained establishment. Also there was a clear need for this work to be carried out in somewhat more private conditions. Tollerton — being a public aerodrome — was hardly a suitable home for modern service aircraft.

"So it was that in December 1934 a couple of 'Belfast' trussed hangars were occupied at RAF Hucknall. The Hawker Hart was flown over from Tollerton to Hucknall and another machine, a Gloster Gnatsnapper II joined the flight complete with Captain R. T. Shepherd who was made full-time Chief Test Pilot together with R. W. Harker, two ground staff engineers and a small support group of technicians. Cyril Lovesay was placed in charge during the initial months until his place was taken by a brilliant and enthusiastic engineer called R. N. Dorey."

Having settled in at Hucknall yet another Hawker Hart arrived (K 1102) and this machine was seized upon as a flying test-bed for radiator experiments as well as having its Kestrel II engine changed for a Kestrel VI. For by this time Rolls Royce engineers were beginning to put into practice some of the new theories concerning aero radiator performance and efficiency. For one thing newer aircraft design shapes to accommodate these radiators — not to mention associated pipework — had to be found; streamlined to minimize drag. An aerodynamics department, a wind tunnel and slave rigs were needed to allow Rolls Royce Limited to move on to another more advanced period of development.

The company was not an aircraft builder as such and thus far had concerned itself with the pursuit of developing and building aero engines along with much associated technical work to make such engines perform better, last longer and, generally, lead the market. That Rolls Royce were achieving this goal of technical perfection was not doubted. The problem was that the aeroplane makers couldn't keep up with the standard of engineering available from Rolls Royce. Their engines were too advanced for the type of airframes then available . . . at least from British makers.

As Colin Gibson put it: "By the end of the first year, 1935, it was evident that with the introduction of new and more powerful engines the slow biplanes with fixed undercarriages and open cockpits were becoming an embarrassment so Rolls Royce started to look around for a more suitable aircraft. To do this they had to go to Germany. There they found the ideal aircraft, a Heinkel He70 — a very robust, passenger carrying all-metal aircraft which the company bought for £13,000 and a Kestrel V engine was sent to Rostock where the German firm carried out the conversion, the plane being flown back to Hucknall by Captain Shepherd on 27 March, 1936."

Rolls Royce technicians and engineers at Hucknall couldn't believe their luck as the aircraft was later thoroughly examined, for the Heinkel was ideal for the kind of work they wanted to carry out. They set to work immediately investigating such things as the effect of radiator positioning on drag, speed, coolant temperatures and much else. In fact this beautiful aeroplane, with its sleek streamlined look, became something of a mascot at Rolls Royce in the three-and-a-half years of its test life up to the outbreak of the Second World War.

And the outcome of experimentation with this aeroplane was something of a turning point for the company who began to adopt the idea of not just building aero engines alone but of putting together a complete power plant; that is to say bolting on all the other necessary parts ready for a unit to be fitted straight into an aircraft. Up to this point Rolls Royce had only been supplying the bare engine . . . from now on they would be selling a more comprehensive product complete with radiators, pipework, aircraft mountings, exhaust systems, cowlings and so on.

A great deal of valuable information had been gained at the

The superb aerodynamic look of the Heinkel HE70. In this 1930s' study the aircraft is about to circle over Hucknall Aerodrome to gain height after take-off. Note the Basford to Bennerley railway line just below the propeller and also the Midland Railway branch curling away from the tail unit towards Watnall Colliery. The present day M1 runs diagonally through the centre of the picture.
Photo: C.T. Gibson

company. The irony from the German point of view at any rate, is that one of their aircraft achieved so much that was very soon to help Rolls Royce and the RAF to maul the *Luftwaffe* over the skies of Southern England in the summer of 1940.

Those balmy and pioneering days of the late 1930s were at an end with the outbreak of hostilities in the autumn of 1939, for Rolls Royce at Hucknall — while still busy with aero engine research and testing — were called upon to help in more immediate ways. Improvements to the famous Merlin engine became one of the most important assignments and this having been achieved some 279 Hurricanes were fitted with uprated power units between September 1940 and April 1941.

A feat of considerable magnitude by any yardstick . . . but the engineers on Watnall Road also managed to squeeze in some 40 similar Spitfire conversions all of which were delivered to the RAF in time for December 1940 by way of a Christmas box!

Contemporary bombers like the Wellington, Whitley and Beaufighter were also fitted with Merlins at Hucknall at this period.

Throughout the war Rolls Royce at Hucknall worked away steadily at a mixed roster of repairing and uprating RAF fighters and continued flight testing and engine development. For example, test flying continued with the Mk II Hurricane aimed at improving

Stan Hart (right) Rolls Royce chief designer at Hucknall with staff in the drawing office.
Photo: C.T. Gibson

engine fuel and 'breathing' efficiency. But many other aircraft types also passed through the workshops — Bristol Beaufighters, Fairey Battles and even, on one occasion, an Avro Manchester.

Britain became famous for many types of aeroplanes, but the Avro Manchester was definitely not one of them. A. V. Roe, who designed it, may not have been entirely at fault since the Rolls Royce 24-cylinder Vulture engine with which it was fitted suffered many problems. In service the Manchester was ill-starred right from the start. Hucknall's link with this plane was disastrous for the flying test-bed had to make an emergency landing in which the pilot was killed. The RAF later replaced the Vulture-powered Avro Manchester with its much more famous Merlin-equipped Lancaster successor.

New, more powerful types of Merlin engine were continually being developed by the company in response to demands from the RAF for faster fighters and heavier bombers. Early 1942, for instance, saw the first flight of the Mark IX Spitfire with a Merlin 60-series intercooled engine and by June 1943 no fewer than 229 such aircraft had been delivered to the RAF. Also during 1942 the first 100-hour extended development flying was completed on the Merlin XX which had been installed in the new Lancaster type. This heavy bomber which became one of the stars of the RAF during the Second World War

Hurricane repair and modification to take a more powerful Merlin engine immediately after the Battle of Britain.
Photo: Stan Grainger/Rolls Royce Heritage

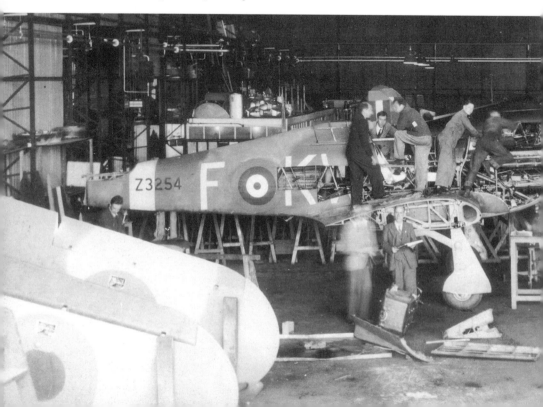

also became the backbone test aircraft for Rolls Royce flight development AFTER the war.

Also in 1942 the RAF were looking to strengthen their fighter squadrons and had an American type sent to their Air Fighting Development Unit (AFDU) at Duxford near Cambridge for evaluation. In the Spring of that year Ronnie Harker, a Rolls Royce test pilot, was invited to Duxford to try this aircraft, the North American Mustang powered by an Allison engine. He returned to Hucknall to praise the handling of this aeroplane and said it had a number of desirable features lacked by the then front line fighters of both sides. But its superb manoeuvrability and low drag were hampered by a low full-throttle height limit from the Allison engine which made its overall performance only suitable for low altitude operation.

Harker, in reply to questions after the flight, stated that the only improvement that could be made would be the installation of a Rolls Royce Merlin engine and after his return to Hucknall he made out a complete reprt together with all the expected performance data in a bid to persuade his superiors to give permission to do just this. They agreed and went one better by allowing five Mustangs to be so converted. This was the start of the story that ended with the

A five-blade Griffon-engined prototype Spitfire at Hucknall probably about 1944/5. Also a Merlin powered MK9 Spitfire keeps it company.
Photo: Stan Grainger/Rolls Royce Heritage

Mustang gaining the reputation for being the greatest piston-engined fighter aircraft of them all . . . and all thanks to that vital finishing touch from the skilled craftsmen and engineers at Hucknall.

In the meantime as the war dragged on the Merlin was unable to be developed further and a new power plant called the Griffon was being introduced and tested in different marques of Spitfire and also in a new type called the Fairey Firefly which was being delivered to the Fleet Air Arm. A. V. Roe were also busy with a new aircraft to replace the ageing Lancaster which metamorphosed as the Avro Shackleton. During the later war years the famous DeHavilland Mosquito was a familiar sight in the Leen Valley skies as Rolls Royce Hucknall had one in which they fitted special Merlins capable of operating at extra-high altitude.

On the other hand wartime plane-spotters might have been alarmed to see the unmistakable silhouette of a German Messerschmitt ME 109 fighter lurking on the clouds over Bulwell. Admittedly this occurred earlier in the war but it does illustrate what a wide range of machines could be seen in the Leen Valley . . . and we've not finished yet! The ME 109 was one that had been shot down and captured reasonably intact. It was sent to Hucknall to be completely stripped and rebuilt. The engine was run up on one of the test-beds for evaluation before being re-united with the airframe when the fighter was flown by Rolls Royce test pilots to gather vital information about its handling and performance for the Air Ministry.

Towards the end of the war a new installation appeared from the company, the 'Universal Power Plant.' These were built at Hucknall and a thousand hours of endurance and pass-off testing was carried out on two special wing hanger test-beds in addition to the flying programmes. Essentially the UPP as it was known was an uprated Merlin, higher powered and intercooled, and was earmarked by AVRO for their new bomber — the Lincoln — which would replace their now-ageing Lancaster. Later the company adopted the UPP for their first post-war civil airliner called the Tudor while the American Douglas company, too, ordered UPP's for their new DC4 airliner. A modified Hucknall based Lancaster DV 199 was the first aircraft to flight test the UPP with an all-up weight of 63,000 lbs (fuel and simulated bomb load) cruising at 30,000 feet.

During the war years, it is interesting to reflect, research and development at Hucknall led to the average speed of Allied fighter aircraft increasing from 360mph to 440mph while the operating ceiling of machines had also been elevated from 32,000 ft. to 45,000 ft. Merlin power was increased dramatically from 1,050 bhp in early engines to 2,050 bhp in later units . . . work that by 1945 had made Hucknall famous. Few other sites in the world could match Rolls Royce Hucknall which had justifiably earned the reputation of being one of the leading experimental and development flight testing establishments in the world. But the jet age was still to come bringing with it new challenges and fresh opportunities for the dedicated and highly skilled team at Rolls Royce.

The start of the 'jet age' at Hucknall was veiled in secrecy with only a handful of people briefed as to what was happening. In August 1942 a Wellington bomber arrived with a strange pointed tail unit where the rear gun turret should have been. However it had a secret experimental engine fitted and this unusual machine carried out a total of nine hours testing. It was simply called the B23 project and no one was allowed to approach the bomber.

But by October of 1943 the jet age was temporarily 'grounded' at Hucknall and the three test aircraft that were by now being used were transferred away. The official reason for this was that Hucknall — with its grass airfield — was unsuitable for this type of testing. It is worth noting, however, that the B23 engine that first took a jet aircraft into the skies and over the Leen Valley was later given the name 'Welland' and in 1945 went into the first jet fighter — the Gloster Meteor which had already been test flying with the Whittle engine installed. This aircraft went into service with the RAF — albeit too late to make any impression on the prosecution of the war effort.

By the time it did enter service with the military the Meteor had the benefit of a new and more powerful development of the Welland unit called the Derwent . . . code named the B37. The technology associated with such things as compressor stall, flame-outs, surging, intakes, turbines and jet pipes was all new and heralded the advent of a new chapter in the history of aviation . . . the jet age.

By 1946 — and with the war in Europe over — the process of disposing of thousands of military aircraft was well under way. The Ministry of Defence no longer had any use for obsolete piston engine fighters so Hurricanes and Spitfires were broken up for they were more valuable as scrap metal . . . although it is said that some were sold just for the residue of fuel in their tanks!

Redundant heavy bombers were even more of a problem to dispose of so Rolls Royce at Hucknall had no problem setting themselves up with half a squadron of the type. Seven Lancaster bombers were based at Hucknall immediately after the end of the war and two of these machines — one the VH742 flying test-bed —

was modified to take the two new Nene jet engines. The two outboard Merlin engines were removed and the Nenes fitted in their place. The first flight on record of such an unusually powered 'Lanc' came in mid-August 1946.

Lancaster - NG 465 - was also 'doctored' to take a new turboprop engine called Dart fitted in the plane's nose and this took to the air in October of that year. Continued development of the engine ended in 1954 when on 22nd January it was written off in a crash-landing on Hollinwell Golf Course. Fortunately there were no casualties but, as we shall see later, not all crews who took off on test flights from Hucknall were so lucky.

Recalled Colin Gibson: "The Nene Lancastrian did a tremendous job for the development of the engine. After take-off the two inboard Merlin engines would be shut down. There were long endurance flights, high altitude tests and engine-handling manoeuvres. The engine had earlier been tried in an American fighter called the Lockheed Shooting Star in July 1945 but its development ended abruptly after an engine failure ended in a crash landing at Syerston in November 1945. The engine was also fitted to a DeHavilland Vampire but because of the small intakes on this aircraft it was not able to develop full engine power and handling was very poor."

The late 1940s proved to be busy times for jet engine development and Rolls Royce Ltd of Hucknall — being at the forefront of the activity — were fully extended. For example a new twin-engine type was being developed by English Electric to become famous in 1950s Britain as the Canberra. This aircraft was powered by a Rolls Royce engine called the Avon — a completely new design of unit with an Axial compressor that was much more powerful than its predecessors.

Avon engine testing continued on the Lancastrian flying test-bed as well as on the Canberra type. Lancastrian VL 970 took to the skies for the first time — with Avons installed — on 16 June, 1949. The new units were fitted in place of the outboard Merlins. This aircraft survived until 1955 when it crashed killing the crew of four.

As new variants of the Avon engine were developed the English Electric Canberra was used extensively to test them . . . for example it was a Canberra that first pioneered the 'Re-heat System' that would be used on the new Lightning fighter being developed by English Electric. Put simply the engine had a modified fuel system which sprayed fuel into specially designed jet pipes where it was ignited to give an engine power boost of between 30% and 40%. The engine and re-heat jet pipes were fitted to a Canberra to develop this installation before the first Lightning flew.

But to carry out these and many other flight tests taking place in the post-war years Hucknall's air faciliites had been forced to expand quite considerably. Six more hangars had appeared and a new tarmac runway laid with a large concrete aircraft park and ground running strip. Special open air test-beds had been built to carry out additional back-up research and to test aerodynamic problems three wind tunnels had been built powered by Derwent and Nene engines. Small models were made and installed in two of the tunnels to test air-flow problems. The third tunnel was employed to investigate the performance of fire extinguisher systems. Here a full-scale engine installation would be rigged complete with a fire extinguisher system. Two Nene engines would be run to create an airflow around the test engine and then the assembly was deliberately set on fire. At the desired moment the fire extinguisher system was activated and its effectiveness monitored.

Other test-beds were used to carry out full scale failure tests of engine compressors and turbines, bird ingestion and noise levels . . . but by the early 1950s a development emerged which would not only bring the Hucknall site to the attention of the aviation world in a big way but which would attract the attention of civvy street, too.

Hucknall people still to this day talk of 'The Flying Bedstead' . . . but they're not necessarily referring to their 'local' in Watnall Road. For there is a pub of that name and to the uninformed it may sound an odd choice of name for a town pub. But the name, itself a popular euphemism for something much more sophisticated and important, derives from a rather unwieldy piece of 'kit' that first took to the air in the town at this period and which had far-reaching implications for the future of modern aircraft; in particular the VTOL principle (Vertical Take-Off and Landing).

As Colin Gibson relates it was a Nene engine which was involved in this very historical event:

"In the early 1950s a very important proposal made by Dr A. A. Griffiths of Rolls Royce started a series of events which had very far-reaching consequences. This was for a jet-borne test-rig for experimental investigation into stability and control concerning vertical thrust using the exhaust gas from a jet engine. This proposal was accepted by the Ministry of Supply and a contract was given to Rolls Royce to build such a vehicle. Its official designation was Thrust Measuring Rig (T.M.R.) but it was soon nicknamed 'The Flying Bedstead.' It was designed by Stan Haert, Chief Installation Designer at Hucknall, and manufacture started in 1952."

Wing Commander Harvey Hayworth, Rolls Royce chief test pilot, takes the 'Flying Bedstead' in the air at Hucknall, circa 1955.
Photo: C.T. Gibson

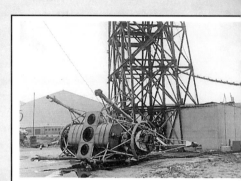

Not all flights were successful. The early 'Bedstead' or Thrust Measuring Rig after an accident in the mid 1950s.

Two Mk4 Nene engines were chosen as fitted to the Sea Hawk aircraft at that time and the only modification required was an air bleed system to allow 10 per cent of the engine compressor air to be bled off for the rig's control system. The engines were fixed facing in opposite directions to each other in a tubular construction with the jet efflux from the jet pipes turned through 90 degrees downwards having one central jet pipe and a bifurcated jet pipe from the other engine.

There were two fuel tanks each holding 95 gallons of fuel fixed below the engines and the whole vehicle was supported by four hydraulic oleo legs. A platform was fitted across the structure above the engines which had a seat bolted to it together with a conventional type control column and rudder pedals. The rig was controlled by bleeding air from the engine through the control valves to diametrically opposed pipes which had nozzles on the end which could swivel 30 degrees in either direction for movement left or right . . . these valves were also interconnected to the control column so that by moving its airflow would be restricted to the nozzles which would thus reduce the thrust thereby controlling the direction of the vehicle.

The thrust to weight ratio of the rig was critical so the research teams at Rolls Royce were careful to keep the machine's weight to a minimum.

For those interested in technicalities each engine gave 3,850 lbs thrust plus 325 lbs thrust from each of the bleed nozzles making a total thrust available of 8,350 lbs. With fuel and 'pilot' on board total weight was 7,196 lbs. But there wasn't much safety margin although one thing in the rig's favour was that after about seven minutes running — just under half its available 'range' — the handling greatly improved.

The Flying Bedstead was given a less colourful appellation by Rolls Royce to whom it was simply . . . XJ314!

First ground run came on 3 July, 1953, basically to run up the engines, test the controls and generally make sure that all was looking promising. Then, three days later, the first attempt at lift-off was made with Wing Commander Harvey Hayworth, Rolls Royce Chief Test Pilot, at the controls. On this occasion the rig merely rose to the full height of the hydraulic oleo legs. The wheels remained on the ground. But it was a stirring start to vertical take off and landing technology although few folk in the area would know for some time of the significance of that important midsummer day in Hucknall.

There were further tests and it was felt early on that for safety's sake the rig should be tethered. A large gantry was built and cables were attached to either side and above the rig from cable drums built into the gantry. Testing then continued with many modifications made to both rig and controls . . . and floor. The blast from the jet engines was so powerful that it was causing the surface to break up!

Finally, in November and after 20 hours' testing, the rig was withdrawn for extensive modifications and overhaul. After a long period in the workshops the rig was eventually rolled out into daylight once more, put under the gantry, and a tethered flight carried out to test the effectiveness of the modifications. They had, as it turned out, been so successful that there was much speculation about a 'free' flight being imminent.

An area out on the airfield hardstanding was prepared complete with a special concrete square and the first flight, by Captain Ron Shepherd, took place on 3 August, 1954, before an audience of specially invited dignitaries. The rig rose slowly into the air and was held steady in a hover attitude. It then moved forward and a circuit of the area was made while sideways and backwards movements were demonstrated before a successful landing was achieved back on the concrete square.

The flight had been a tremendous success and during the next four months a number of additional free flights were made all at a height of between 13 and 15 feet although one test flight did rise to 50 feet to ensure that the rig's performance was not being affected by the ground. The final flight took place on 15 December, 1954, after which the rig was transferred to Farnborough.

Another was built in 1955 but had a far less illustrious career than its predecessor. The second rig was numbered XK126 and this carried out extensive tethered flying tests before making its first free flight on 12 November, 1956. This rig crashed a year later at the end of November 1957 killing the pilot.

Colin Gibson suggests that after successfully proving Dr. Griffiths' theory of vertical thrust, Rolls Royce went away from this idea and pursued their own ideas of small jet engines for vertical lift later to be demonstrated by the Short SC1 aircraft. To develop these small engines two Gloster Meteor aircraft were modified to flight test them. One had a small Soar engine fitted to a wing tip and a dummy engine to the other. The second aeroplane had an RB108 engine installed vertically in the fuselage behind the pilot.

Meanwhile the development of the Avon engine continued at Hucknall with a view to its installation into two new fighter types — the Hawker Hunter and Supermarine Swift. Examples of both aircraft arrived in the Leen Valley for development.

Recalls Colin: "The Hunter was very manoeuvrable and easy to fly and the RAF used them in their aerobatic display team. With later and more powerful versions of the Avon engine fitted this became the RAF's front line fighter before the arrival of the new supersonic English Electric Lightning with the re-heat jet pipe system which had been tested on the Canberra.

"One of the Hunters was modified to test another jet pipe system that had been designed to reduce landing distances. This was called a thrust reverser and was achieved by fitting clamshell doors in the jet pipe to close and reverse the jet efflux to blow forwards through two outlets in the fuselage AFTER landing. Considerable development on this component was carried out at Hucknall. This was later refined into a complete 'bolt-on' unit which was then used on all future civil airliners together with noise suppression jet pipe nozzles which had also been tested on the special open air test-beds."

Work was also going on to enhance the Dart turboprop engine and as was Rolls Royce policy an 'old timer' was called into service to assist as a flying test-bed. Instead of a pensioned-off Lancaster, though, the choice this time was a Douglas DC3 Dakota — a type developed in pre-war America that was, and still is, the most prolific

Wreckage of Canberra bomber which crashed on railway sidings at Bulwell after losing power on one engine just after take off.
Photo: Stan Grainger/Rolls Royce Heritage

and longlived aircraft type of all time. In any case the supply of airworthy Lancasters would no doubt have been drying up by now.

Two Dart turboprop engines were fitted to the Dakota in place of the plane's original radial power plants. Subsequent trials were so successful that another similar aircraft was similarly modified and flown by British European Airways as a freighter.

Meanwhile an even larger and more powerful turboprop engine called the Tyne had been installed in the nose of an Avro Lincoln and this project again enjoyed great success to the extent that continuing development on both engine types could only be continued with the aid of more test-bed aircraft. Two more machines were acquired. The first was a civil twin-engine airliner, the Airspeed Ambassador, which was fitted with two uprated Dart engines and this was joined by an Elizabethan which was equipped with two Tyne engines. Both types of power unit subsequently became world class aero engines finding employment with countless operators on both short and long haul airfreight and airliner work.

Another engine type which was flight tested at Hucknall and developed by Rolls Royce was the Gazelle Free Power turbine which was installed in the Westland Wessex helicopter. For this project Rolls Royce had to excavate a large pond! But it wasn't a departure into

This Vulcan lost a wing over RAF Newton in the 1950s. Based at Hucknall it had minutes earlier passed over the town. A visitor watching the airshow gave the picture to Rolls Royce. Photo: Stan Grainger/Rolls Royce Heritage

leisure time angling that prompted this odd break from aero engines . . . the helicopter was hovered above the water to see what spray ingestion damage might occur to the engine. The idea was to agitate the water to simulate marine conditions.

But by far the largest pure jet engine Rolls Royce developed — the Conway — started its flight development at Hucknall. It was installed as a complete Pod power plant slung beneath the fuselage of an Avro development airliner called the Ashton which was a modified Tudor aircraft powered by four Nene jet engines.

Also one of the hanger test-beds was completely modified from piston engine to jet engine testing. A complete Pod power plant and aircraft pylon was installed to provide development for a new American Boeing 707 airliner and hundreds of hours of endurance testing was carried out in conjuncion with the flight development being pursued on the Ashton. The Conway unit was also developed for fitting to the RAF Victor bomber, an example of which spent time at Hucknall as trials progressed.

The so-called 'Cold War' years of the 1950s and early 1960s saw many strange and yet impressive military aircraft take to the skies and Rolls Royce at Hucknall were more often than not the firm entrusted with the business of helping in the design, testing and commissioning of the new generation jet engines . . . many people living within a mile or so of Hucknall Aerodrome will testify to the sound effects so created.

The Handley Page Victor was an excellent example of the new breed of 1950s modern jet-powered bomber. But there can be no doubt that the Avro company's Vulcan stole the limelight much as its predecessor the Lancaster had in the previous wartorn decade.

It was the Vulcan which was selected to assist in the continuing development of the Conway engine along with yet another new Rolls Royce power plant called the Spey. At the same time the Wing Hanger test-bed was modified once more to test this newcomer. The sight of an Avro Vulcan became common in the local skies . . . in the late 1950s the author, as a schoolboy, lived in Arnold and the test Vulcan regularly sailed through the clouds over Redhill on its approach to a landing at Hucknall . . . the appearance of this enormous ivory-coloured delta wing bomber aircraft was striking to say the least!

Hundreds of hours of endurance testing were carried out on the Spey with the engine running night and day before being fitted to two new civil aircraft, the Trident and BAC 1-11. The Trident was powered by three engines installed at the rear of the fuselage with the centre engine intake being a completely new design.

As invariably happened the Spey engine was again uprated and, in a more powerful guise with a very advanced re-heat jet pipe system, was tested and installed in an American Phantom — an achievement which owed a great deal to earlier pioneering work on the English Electric Lightning.

Finally the largest Conway engine ever built — the RC042/43 — powered the large four-engine VC10 airliner. Hopes that this engine would be taken up by the former British Overseas Airways Corporations (BOAC) were frustrated by the Corporation's decision to move to Boeing 747's so only a handful of VC10's were built.

Colin Gibson recalls: "An engine of this size was very costly on fuel consumption and noisy as well so a complete new design of fuel efficient/low noise capability unit was required which gave rise to the first 'fan' engine more widely known as the RB 211. Nothing had been seen like it before. It was new technology indeed! The fan blades were made of carbon fibre for lightness. This was a specially formulated material made at Hucknall and, to monitor this engine, two brand new open-air test-beds had to be built and one of them became the Rolls Royce master performance thrust and noise bed

English Electric Lightning at Hucknall. Jim Hayworth, Rolls Royce test pilot takes out a vintage Austin. The passenger is Jimmy Jackson from Canada. The car belonged to a young Derby Avon engine engineer. Circa 1960.
Photo: Stan Grainger/Rolls Royce Heritage

against which all other beds were calibrated. The other bed was used to carry out special slave installation tests where thrust and engine performance were not required.

It is a matter of some significance that things went awry only very, very infrequently at Hucknall which is quite an achievement when one considers that technicians and engineers were quite literally working on the outermost fringes of aviation technology. Unfortunately crashes — particularly aeroplane crashes — do tend to attract attention often, therefore giving a distorted impression of air safety to the general public.

Although not strictly speaking a flying accident the testing of the RB 211 did encounter a very serious 'failure' when, during a test with the engine running at full power, all the carbon fibre fan blades shredded and blew the front of the engine off. Fortunately nobody was hurt in this incident but it was a big setback for the development programme . . . the future of this new technology fan had come to an end so Rolls Royce had to retreat and fall back on metal blades, reliable but much heavier.

A BAC VC10 had been chosen to test fly the new engine and the twin-port Conway engines were removed from the fuselage and an RB211 pod installed at Hucknall. The first test flight was made in 1970 . . . but in March the following year it was announced that all flying from Rolls Royce at Hucknall would cease and on 8 March, 1972, the very last flying test-bed aircraft flew out of the Leen Valley. In future test flying would be carried out from Bristol.

With the effective closure of Hucknall as an airbase the district lost something of its special atmosphere; for there was never anything nor any place quite like Hucknall Aerodrome for the sheer variety of aircraft types that could be seen coming and going whether on RAF or Rolls Royce business. In the 1960s for example, it was still possible to wander down Farley's Lane to the end of the runway in those pre-bypass days and sit and watch an airshow without paying! Engine testing continues at Hucknall to this day.

If your interest was in trains as well as aircraft then you were well catered for since the raised embankment conveying the former Great Central Railway tracks passed across the bottom end of the runway and when there was a lull in aircraft activity one might turn one's attention to the sight of a D.11 4-4-0 steam engine rattling past from Sheffield to Nottingham with a five-coach stepping train.

Although mainstream flying ceased in the early 1970s part of the airfield (though not the main runway) is still used by the Merlin Flying Club and from time to time flying rallies bring many 'foreign' light aircraft into the skies around Bulwell and Hucknall.

The 'golden years' of aviation in the Leen Valley may have gone for ever but the spirit of flight lives on as elderly piston-engine biplanes and monoplanes still bounce to their landings in those fields once owned by the Duke of Portland.

Modern technology. Engine power plant testing facilities at Hucknall. Results are relayed to Derby . . . power for airliners in the 21st century.
Photo: Stan Grainger/Rolls Royce Heritage

GERARDS

Millions of people have over the years washed with soap made at a Leen Valley factory or otherwise freshened themselves up with one or other of the products from the former Gerard Brothers Ltd. works in Wilkinson Street, Basford. This 1930s view shows employees at work in the company's packing room. Famous for its Imperial Leather soap, Gerard Brothers Ltd. was founded in 1867 by Thomas and William Gerard and by the early 1960's Gerards was said to be the most technically advanced soap works in the world. Earlier in 1955 the whole of the share capital of Gerards was bought by Cussons Sons & Co. Ltd. of Manchester.

Photos: Nottinghamshire County Council Leisure Services

RALEIGH

The name Raleigh became synonymous with cycling around the world and millions of riders have pedalled on machines built at the Leen Valley's biggest factory. During the Second World War the factory was turned over to munitions work but in the 1940s and 1950s Raleigh enjoyed a boom and acquired famous brand names like Carlton, BSA, Triumph and Rudge. At this time the factory spread over 40 acres and employed more than 8,000. The original company started in 1890 three years after founder Sir Frank Bowden acquired a small bicycle works in Raleigh Street.

Photo: Nottinghamshire County Council Leisure Services

JAMES SHIPSTONE & SONS

James Shipstone & Sons, Star Brewery, New Basford. Long after lorries took over delivering the Shipstone's brew to local pubs the company continued to operate a horse-drawn dray which no doubt was a splendid marketing and public relations ploy. People used to enjoy the spectacle even though some never touched a glass of ale! To generations of Leen Valley drinkers a pint of 'Shippo's' was nectar. The New Basford brewery created what many felt to be THE taste of Nottingham.

In its heyday the brewery of James Shipstone & Sons in Radford Road cultivated an intensely loyal and enthusiastic patronage kept happily supplied via a network of mainly working-class hostelries in and around the city.

New Basford and district, in particular, gave the impression of having a Shipstones pub or off-sales on just about every street corner. The New Basford brew could be tasted further afield and in common with other Nottingham area breweries, Shipstones was sold at, and on the way to, the popular east coat holiday resorts. But by and large Shipstones was, really, THE drink of Nottingham and the majority of its outlets remained local . . . as did its customers.

Certainly New Basford will never again experience the combined aroma of brewery, gas works and soap factory, something which added to the character of this part of the district!

Photo: Nottinghamshire County Council Leisure Services

WILFORD POWER STATION

The River Trent rather than the Leen is featured in this view of Wilford Power Station which, for sheer size, took some beating. This colossal generating station vanished from the scene in the early 1970s and with it went the remains of Clifton Colliery the headstocks of which can be seen sprouting from the roof of the Nottingham City Transport double decker on the right of the picture. Then and now, anglers found the Trent a pleasant retreat in spite of the close proximity of such industry. The site is now a retail park.

Photo: Nottinghamshire County Council Leisure Services

JOHN PLAYER & SONS

Leenside Nottingham suburbs like Hyson Green and Radford were spared Basford's experience of gas works' smells but instead had the aroma of Virginia tobacco wafting out of the Player's factory. Players' origins go back to the year 1877 when Mr. John Player took over a small existing tobacco business in the city. He became the pioneer of the pre-packed tobacco trade. Player's Navy Cut was born. John Player & Sons grew to become one of Nottinghamshire's major employers providing 7,000 jobs in the 1930s. In 1901 the Imperial Tobacco Company (of Great Britain and Ireland) Ltd. was formed to protect British trade from an attack then being made upon it by American manufacturers. This 1930s' view inside the Radford factory shows young ladies packing cigarettes.

Photo: Nottingham County Council Leisure Services.